ARHOOLIE Records

DOWN HOME MUSIC

The Stories and Photographs of Chris Strachwitz

BY **JOEL SELVIN** WITH **CHRIS STRACHWITZ**

CHRONICLE BOOKS
SAN FRANCISCO

Copyright © 2023 by The Arhoolie Foundation.

All rights reserved. No part of this book may be reproduced in any form without written permission from the publisher.

Library of Congress Cataloging-in-Publication Data available.

ISBN 978-1-7972-2228-8

Manufactured in China.

All photographs by Chris Strachwitz except pages 19–57: unless indicated, photographers are unknown.

Design by Jon Glick.

Frontmatter photo captions: pp. 2–3: Lightnin' Hopkins, 1964, Houston, Texas; pp. 4–5: Fred McDowell, 1965, Como, Mississippi; pp. 6–7: A house in southern Mississippi, 1968; pp. 8–9: Los Pingüinos del Norte, 1970, Piedras Negras, Coahuila, Mexico; pp. 10–11: Casa's, 1986, San Antonio, Texas; pp. 12–13: Marc and Ann Savoy with Michael Doucet, 1982, Eunice, Louisiana

10 9 8 7 6 5 4 3 2 1

Chronicle books and gifts are available at special quantity discounts to corporations, professional associations, literacy programs, and other organizations. For details and discount information, please contact our premiums department at corporatesales@chroniclebooks.com or at 1-800-759-0190.

Chronicle Books LLC
680 Second Street
San Francisco, California 94107
www.chroniclebooks.com

Contents

BEEN HERE, DONE GONE

THE MUSICAL JOURNEYS OF CHRIS STRACHWITZ

BY JOEL SELVIN

IN SEPTEMBER 1971, the Muddy Waters band came to San Francisco for a few nights at the North Beach rock and blues club Keystone Korner. Chris Strachwitz of Arhoolie Records watched the funky Oakland bluesman L. C. "Good Rockin'" Robinson sit in with the band, playing his Hawaiian steel guitar with the Chicago blues masters, while another blues great, John Lee Hooker, grunted approval on vocals. It occurred to Strachwitz that the Waters band would make excellent accompanists for a record with L. C., and he struck a deal to take them all in the studio the next afternoon.

L. C. Robinson was unlikely to attract any other record company interest. He had recently retired from his work in a laundry, as the steam had aggravated his bursitis. He lived in genteel poverty with his wife, Peggy, on disability insurance in a small Berkeley house where the living room was dominated by a velvet painting of John and Robert Kennedy and Martin Luther King Jr. His few gigs were limited to ghetto clubs with tiny audiences. The fifty-seven-year-old bluesman had never achieved any real notoriety in a career that stretched back decades. Strachwitz knew him from an obscure 1945 78 RPM record on the Black & White label made with his harmonica-playing brother and released under the name "the Robinson Brothers." He had been banging around the edges of the East Bay blues scene virtually ever since, this eccentric steel guitarist who was an offbeat-enough blues musician to elicit the attention of Strachwitz.

For the previous ten years, Strachwitz had been rummaging through the dusty corners of American music—blues, country, traditional jazz, even Mexican American folk music—for his Arhoolie Records, where he had discovered scores of musicians who would have otherwise disappeared into the bayou mists from where they came. Arhoolie, in fact, was likely the only record label that would have the slightest interest in L. C.

Having obtained world-class players for the session, Strachwitz booked time at San Francisco's Wally Heider Studios, where rock bands like Jefferson Airplane, Santana, Creedence Clearwater, and Crosby, Stills, Nash & Young made their records. As

CHRIS AT HIS HOUSE RECORDING JUKE BOY BONNER 1972, BERKELEY, CALIFORNIA

Chris recorded a lot of the early Arhoolie Records in his Berkeley hills living room.
Photo by Tony Ray-Jones.

someone who cut most of his albums on a portable tape recorder, he did not customarily rent such high-end facilities for his down home productions. When the band arrived to set up instruments and prepare for the session, they came with a surprise bonus: Muddy Waters himself.

With his guys on the session, the great Waters, dignified and austere, took charge of the room, directing where the players should place themselves and watching over them as they warmed up. From the control room, Strachwitz beamed with pleasure over this unexpected assistance. Charlie Musselwhite, whose Arhoolie solo album made him the label's bestselling act (at more than three thousand copies), came along to play harmonica. Waters stalked the room as the band charged into the first take, using hand signals to direct the action, even going so far as to point to the fret on the guitarist's neckboard where he wanted him to start his solo. He knew his musicians intimately, and his masterful command was like watching Duke Ellington preside over a rehearsal.

It wasn't until after the second number, with a warm feeling of accomplishment threading through the room, that L. C. pulled out a bottle of vodka. But passing it around had an almost immediate deleterious effect on the session. On the next number, L. C. was having trouble switching from playing his steel guitar to the fiddle, and Waters, clearly disgusted at the drunken display, slipped quietly out of the room to return to his hotel and wash his hands of the affair.

In the control booth, Strachwitz teetered on his heels, hands in pockets, trying to marshal some direction to the session, which was slipping away as L. C. and the other musicians grew ever more intoxicated. He grinned a crooked smile and soldiered on until the afternoon wound down, glad to have captured at least four or five usable tracks. By the end of the session, the musicians were all trashed. But it could have been worse, and Strachwitz had grown accustomed to navigating obstacles other record producers would never even encounter.

Chris Strachwitz thinks of himself not as a record producer but as a song catcher. He belongs firmly in the tradition of Cecil Sharp, the British musicologist who collected hundreds of Elizabethan folk songs during World War I in the West Virginia hills. He is the modern descendant of John and Alan Lomax, the intrepid pioneers who made field recordings of Leadbelly, Woody Guthrie, and dozens of others for the Library of Congress. He entered the record business as a means to support his passion; he only made money by accident. *San Francisco Chronicle* jazz and pop critic Ralph J. Gleason told Strachwitz that he didn't have a record company—he had a hobby. He frequently found himself in confounding and complicated circumstances when it came to making his records with these remarkable musicians.

In the course of more than forty years behind the one-man operation, Strachwitz became the single most important and formidable folklorist of his generation. He not only brought to light important American blues musicians such as Lightnin' Hopkins, Mississippi Fred McDowell, Mance Lipscomb, and zydeco king Clifton Chenier, he rescued the vast and rich legacy of Texas-Mexican norteño music, even though he barely speaks a word of Spanish. He has recorded blues in Chicago, Cajun music in the Louisiana bayous, bluegrass in Appalachia, Mexican music in Texas barrios. He has retrieved hundreds of important forgotten records from the past and restored them to the literature. There has not been a single corner of the sweeping panorama of American music he has not explored or an important trend or discovery in American vernacular music over the past fifty years that does not bear his fingerprints.

Strachwitz made records like a documentary filmmaker: crisp, dry recordings designed to feature the performance and the repertoire. He never washed his tracks in reverb or other effects. He didn't spend infinite hours performing intricate, detailed mixes. He didn't bring arrangers, supporting musicians, or other professional assistance into making his records. He was producing aural documents of the music, and the more real it sounded, the better. Because of this, his records stand up through the years; they sound as fresh and vital as the day they were first captured.

All through his adventures in recording this music, Strachwitz also brought a camera. As he didn't think of himself as a record producer, neither did he consider himself a photographer. He brought the used Leica 35 mm camera he bought in Germany when he was in the army in the early '50s to take snapshots. To him, the camera was nothing more than a utilitarian tool to make album cover photos and perhaps portraits for publicity. As with his records, his simple intent belied the skill and keen perspective Strachwitz brought to his photography. Because of his intimate knowledge of the people he photographed and what they did, he knew what to shoot. He knew how to pose the people, and he could capture the candid moments. He understood what to include in the composition and how to tell a story in a single frame. As with his records, his photographs document an incredible journey through American music from his special vantage point with his knowing eye.

He was born July 1, 1931, as Christian Alexander Maria, Graf Strachwitz von Gross-Zauche und Camminetz, in Gross Reichenau, Lower Silesia, then within Germany and now known as Bogaczów, Poland. His family were aristocratic farm owners, although his grandmother had been born in San Francisco, the daughter of US senator Francis Newlands of Nevada. Count Strachwitz never uses his title. "Over here," he says, "it doesn't count."

Young Strachwitz's lifelong fascination with records began with a record the family owned of a song from an old operetta, "Die Berliner Luft" (The Berlin Air). He listened to it repeatedly, until his father warned him not to play the record. The songwriter was Jewish, he told the ten-year-old boy, and the Nazis might not like it. Strachwitz learned early on that listening to music was not necessarily an innocent pleasure, yet he never lost his fascination with records.

After the war and two years at an uncle's house in the British zone, his family was invited to immigrate to the United States by two great-aunts, one of whom offered her large home in Reno, Nevada. The sixteen-year-old was sent to boarding school. Strachwitz first encountered the many sounds of American music on late-night radio. The laments of hillbilly singers and bluesmen resonated with the shy, young immigrant who felt like a stranger in a strange land and related to the outsider appeal of these rural musicians, who clearly took no part in mainstream American life.

His musical education continued as he attended the exclusive Cate School in Southern California, where the 1947 movie *New Orleans* with Louis Armstrong, the full Kid Ory band, and Billie Holiday made a big impression on the gawky, awkward teen. He started collecting records. In 1952, he first heard the traditional New Orleans jazz master George Lewis and his band on a daylong Dixieland jamboree at the Shrine Auditorium in

Los Angeles, on a bill with a batch of square bands playing what Strachwitz would come to call "Mickey Mouse music." But George Lewis was the real deal. The clarinet player whose career went back to the '20s was a leading figure in the ongoing New Orleans jazz revival at the time, an authentic link to the music's storied past.

While attending Pomona College, he schooled himself in the rich variety of American music on the margins of society—country, jazz, gospel, and blues. He first heard Texas bluesman Lightnin' Hopkins on Hunter Hancock's *Harlem Matinee* on Los Angeles radio, and he was enraptured by the singer's grizzled, ageless voice. Hopkins became his favorite blues singer and a touchstone for everything that would follow.

Strachwitz visited Dolphin's of Hollywood, a twenty-four-hour, seven-day-a-week record store in the heart of South Central Los Angeles that served as much as a cultural center to the Black community as a music store. They did not see that many white customers, and when Chris asked if they had anything by Lightnin' Hopkins, the saleslady went into shock. "You like those down home blues?" she said.

After finishing college, two years in the army, and earning credentials at UC Berkeley, Strachwitz was teaching German in a public school in Los Gatos, a small town amid fruit orchards an hour's drive south of San Francisco, when he received the postcard that would change his life.

The world of blues enthusiasts was quite small at the time, and Strachwitz had met fellow blues scholar Sam Charters in Berkeley some years before, when Charters was working on the first book on the subject, *The Country Blues*. On the postcard, Charters wrote that he had located the elusive blues singer Lightnin' Hopkins in Houston. Hopkins, whose recording career had cooled considerably, was a mysterious figure to these arcane record collectors, who knew little of his background or even where he lived. To Strachwitz, this was monumental news that would prove to be life changing. In summer 1959, as soon as school let out, the twenty-eight-year-old public school teacher hightailed it to Texas to see bluesman Lightnin' Hopkins.

That rainy night in Houston, on a trip he would later describe as "a pilgrimage," where Chris first heard Lightnin' in a low-rent Third Ward beer joint called Pop's Place, the legendary bluesman ad-libbed his way through a recitation of the evening's difficulties—bad weather, car trouble on the way to the club, aches in his joints—winding up by noting, "And this man come all the way from California just to hear po' Lightnin' play." This was Strachwitz's road-to-Damascus moment. His life would never be the same.

For the next thirty years or so, Strachwitz would document his travels with a tape recorder and a camera. As he assembled his vast library of field and studio recordings of indigenous American musicians, he collected a reservoir of photographs along the way that unwittingly chronicled his deep journey into the heart of American music. It all began with his fascination with Lightnin' Hopkins.

Back-to-Texas Summer *(1960)*

THE NEXT SUMMER, Strachwitz packed his Japanese tape recorder in the car trunk and headed back to Texas, intent on capturing in its natural habitat some of this music that fired his imagination so vividly. In Navasota, Texas, he was introduced to Mance

CHRIS WITH LIGHTNIN' HOPKINS AND LUKE "LONG GONE" MILES
1959, HOUSTON, TEXAS

On Chris's first day in Houston and first meeting Lightnin' Hopkins.

Lipscomb, a recently retired fieldworker and sharecropper who had never left his home-town, and Chris recorded the sixty-five-year-old songster and guitarist at his house in a session that would become the first of some four hundred albums Chris would make for his landmark Arhoolie Records.

Strachwitz knew Paul Oliver through correspondence with the British blues authority who had been writing about the music for British jazz magazines since 1952. Since Big Bill Broonzy first brought the blues to Britain in 1955, English jazz fans had developed an appetite for the American music not shared by many back in the States. Oliver raised money for an American trip through the BBC and the US State Department and made plans to meet Strachwitz in Memphis and tour the South. He sent a lengthy list of potential contacts he wanted to meet. In June 1960, after school was out, Strachwitz

CHRIS WITH WAYNE POST
1961, BERKELEY, CALIFORNIA

Chris and graphic artist Wayne
Post paste covers on the first
Arhoolie album, *Mance Lipscomb:*
Texas Songster.

drove to Texas with a friend from Santa Clara, Bob Pinson, who went as far as Dallas, where he planned to interview Western Swing veterans of the Bob Wills bands.

In Dallas, Strachwitz found Lil Son Jackson in an old phone book in the library and located the original singer of the blues classic "Rock Me Baby" working in an auto parts store, long gone from the music business. On the advice of a Berkeley music store owner, Strachwitz had brought along a guitar and, indeed, Jackson no longer owned an instrument. He was reluctant to record and was accustomed to being paid a hundred dollars per song, far beyond what Strachwitz's meager resources would allow.

In the meantime, Mack McCormick, who had been Strachwitz's host on his pilgrimage to see Lightnin' Hopkins the previous year, suggested they drive up to Washington County to look for Tom Moore, subject of a Lightnin' Hopkins song, "Tom Moore's Farm." Moore kept an office over the bank building in downtown Navasota, and after they asked if he knew any guitar players, Moore directed them to the railroad station, where a fellow called Peg Leg sent them on the highway out of town to a small place owned by Mance Lipscomb. When he returned home that afternoon, June 30, 1960, the kindly retired sharecropper found these two strange white men waiting on his porch, one a tall, gangly gent with a pronounced German accent. They asked him to sing some blues and handed him the guitar Strachwitz brought. He played them "St. Louis Blues"—not exactly what they had in mind.

Lipscomb, they would discover, was not a classic blues artist, but a songster—someone who had devoted to memory hundreds of songs. His repertoire spanned old pop songs, polkas, waltzes, ballads, and, yes, blues. At first, Strachwitz was somewhat disappointed, but McCormick understood immediately what they had discovered. "This is what Leadbelly was to the Lomaxes," he told Strachwitz.

As the afternoon stretched into the evening and the dialogue grew more relaxed and convivial, Strachwitz began rolling tape as Lipscomb sang song after song into his recorder. Outside of a couple of experiments with the equipment in Berkeley, this was Strachwitz's first field recording session. He had no idea that he had captured a treasure of American folklore. But he had.

Back and forth between Dallas and Houston, Strachwitz spent as much time as he could with Lightnin' Hopkins. McCormick was trying to represent the blues singer in some kind of business capacity, but Strachwitz didn't feel ready to record his idol, and Lightnin' wasn't looking at Strachwitz that way. Strachwitz drank in the atmosphere around Lightnin', fascinated with that whole life.

He bounced through New Orleans en route to meet Paul Oliver in Memphis. On his way, he found the Hodges Brothers, hillbilly singers he knew from an old 78, outside Bogue Chito, Mississippi, living with their mother in a one-room shack, so poor they didn't have a henhouse and their chickens roosted in the trees. He took them to the local radio station, where they broadcast a weekly show, and recorded them.

In Memphis, he met up with Oliver and his wife, Valerie, where Oliver eagerly conducted interviews with old jug band musicians. They headed off into the South, Oliver's wife crammed in the back seat of Strachwitz's two-door coupe next to boxes of old records they collected. In Clarksdale, Mississippi, they met with barber and local blues aficionado Wade Walton, who showed them around town only to have Strachwitz with his California plates pulled over by local constabulary, who let him go after they saw the old records in the car and warned him not to drive any Black people around in his car in the future, although not in exactly those words.

At Walton's barbershop, Strachwitz captured some remarkable impromptu blues from one Robert Curtis Smith, while Walton kept time with his razor strop. In Zachary, Louisiana, they did some recording with Butch Cage and Willie Thomas, a Mutt and Jeff pair of backwoods string band musicians who had been recorded by folklorist Harry Oster. In Hollandale, Mississippi, they caught up with sixty-three-year-old Sam Chatmon, who recorded extensively during the '30s as a member of the Mississippi Sheiks but had been working on a plantation the past twenty years, where they recorded his standout number "I Have to Paint My Face."

Back in Dallas, they located Whistlin' Alex Moore, who made his first record in 1929 and had not recorded again since the late '30s, but he did not own a piano. After rejecting several bars in the Central Track district where Moore occasionally played, they eventually found a local piano teacher who had an appropriate instrument and recorded him there. Moore was greatly amused by the lanky, smiling German and his fussy British associate. These were not the kind of white people these Black musicians were used to seeing.

They went back to Lil Son Jackson, came to terms with him, and recorded him in his apartment using Strachwitz's guitar. They returned to Navasota for a second session with Mance Lipscomb. They also managed to meet Black Ace, another Texas bluesman from the '30s who had not played music since he served in the army during World War II. Again, these unusual European gentlemen were able to convince him to sing for Strachwitz's tape recorder.

They had covered thousands of miles on highways and state roads, crisscrossing the American South in search of genuine, vernacular music, as Strachwitz tuned the radio in to evangelist preacher broadcasts until both the Olivers begged him to stop. Strachwitz drove home in August with his back seat and trunk stuffed with old records and his tapes.

That November, he and graphic artist Wayne Pope sat at a kitchen table and pasted covers on the first 250 copies of the first album on Arhoolie Records, *Texas Songster* by Mance Lipscomb. Mack McCormick suggested the label's name, thinking it was a term for field hollers, and Pope designed the guitar-shaped logo. Strachwitz took the album around to several Berkeley record stores around the campus, and he and Arhoolie Records were in business.

MANCE COMES WEST; BACK TO THE SOUTH *(1961-1962)*

IN FALL 1962, Strachwitz quit teaching school and moved to Berkeley after spending a few weeks sleeping at Jack's Record Cellar in San Francisco, the tiny, one-man outfit that was distributing the Arhoolie albums. He needed to be closer to the center of the action. Strachwitz was getting by on his savings, selling old blues records overseas and on the few pennies he could scrape up from the record label.

Two years on, Arhoolie had more than a half dozen albums in the market. In addition to the Mance Lipscomb long-player, which had been favorably noticed by *Saturday Review* and had caused a modest ripple in folk circles, he made albums from his Texas trip with Alex Moore, Lil Son Jackson, and Black Ace. He recorded a fierce album in his Los Gatos cabin in October 1960 with Big Joe Williams, fresh out of jail on an assault charge, having been introduced to the bluesman responsible for the original "Baby Please Don't Go" by Bob Geddins, a veteran lone cat record producer on the Oakland blues scene. Geddins, who ran a variety of labels and recorded many blues acts, including Lowell Fulson, Jimmy McCracklin, Sugar Pie DeSanto, and others around Oakland since World War II, showed the goofy young German some of the ropes, gave him advice, and encouraged him.

In April 1961, Strachwitz made an album with the classic blues piano man Mercy Dee, whose primal 1953 hit "One Room Country Shack" had been one of his favorites, renting time in a studio in Stockton, California, near where the pianist lived, and a Berkeley recording studio. By the time he relocated to Berkeley, Arhoolie Records was a full-time obsession for Strachwitz.

The Berkeley he moved into was a burbling cauldron of musical, social, and political changes. The University of California campus dominated the landscape, and new ideas and new attitudes were part of Berkeley life, the early rumblings of the coming counterculture. Poets and folk singers could sometimes be heard at the Blind Lemon, a San Pablo Avenue beatnik bar. The Jabberwock on Telegraph Avenue featured a steady stream of folk music; guitarist John Fahey was a regular. Strachwitz preferred the Cabale on San Pablo Avenue, where the musical fare ran more toward the down home sound he craved.

This kind of music was a passion for a growing underground outside of nightclubs and the occasional concert. A small community surrounded this quietly burgeoning scene. Strachwitz frequently dragged his recording gear to music parties at the home of Dave Fredrickson, a Berkeley-born singer who loved to share songs with other musicians sitting around his living room, where fresh, young voices mingled with wizened elders. Phil Huffman operated a kind of folk music salon and rooming house for out-of-town fellow travelers like Sonny Terry and Brownie McGhee, who always stayed there when they were in town. Bob Dylan once brought Joan Baez to Thanksgiving dinner at the Huffmans', anxious to make the acquaintance of Mance Lipscomb, another regular Huffman house guest. At the time, Berkeley was an incubator of many things.

Mance Lipscomb, meanwhile, took the train from Texas to perform at the Jubilee Concert of the Berkeley Folk Festival on the Fourth of July weekend 1961 before a capacity crowd of more than ten thousand people. Amid folk music royalty such as Jean Ritchie and Sam Hinton, the auspicious debut of Mance Lipscomb, who had never performed before any kind of a paid audience, was the high point of the weekend. Mance treated the occasion with his uncommon aplomb and dignity. He had already lived his life, worked the fields, retired, and expected to live out his life quietly in Navasota, never dreaming of anything like this. From here on out, everything would be an unexpected bonus that he greeted with warmth and generosity, somehow remaining miraculously unchanged by his great fortune but always grateful.

Although his 1961 trip south that summer would not yield anything like the epic results of his previous year's tour, Strachwitz would continue to have his eyes opened to the wide and varied possibilities of American music. It was on this trip that he first encountered the lively Louisiana Creole music that some people called zydeco, although mostly it was known simply as French music. This accordion-driven dance music captivated Strachwitz in the Houston beer joints where these musicians played. He recorded Albert Chevalier and Good Rockin' Sam at MacGowan's Lounge, and Willie Green at Irene's Bar, catching the music in its moment.

The Mance Lipscomb album had brought Strachwitz to the attention of the folk music world and Prestige Records. The New York label delved deeply into folk music and hired him to make an album with Robert Curtis Smith, whom he had recorded in Wade Walton's barbershop in Clarksdale the summer before. He took Smith into the historic Sun Studio of Memphis, Tennessee, where Sam Phillips had recorded Elvis Presley, Johnny Cash, Carl Perkins, and Jerry Lee Lewis. In fact, Elvis's guitar player Scotty Moore served as engineer on the sessions and volunteered to play drums on one track. If Strachwitz knew the background of his illustrious sideman, he made no note of it in his recording log. "Engineer plays drums," he wrote.

His own recordings on this trip were limited due to equipment malfunction. His imported Roberts tape recorder crapped out, overmodulated, and ruined most of the recordings. If that wasn't enough, a proposed dream date with his blues hero Lightnin'

Hopkins in Houston went awry after the bluesman and Mack McCormick got into a disagreement over Lightnin's fees that almost came to blows. Not all his field trips would be equally successful, Strachwitz was learning.

When his field recordings didn't produce results, Strachwitz turned to licensing other people's recordings for Arhoolie. He obtained rights to great early recordings by Lowell Fulson (originally done with Bob Geddins) and Big Joe Turner with Pete Johnson's Orchestra from the Swing Time label. He bought thirty acetates for $300 recorded in 1947 with Guitar Slim and Jelly Belly.

That fall, he returned to the South, where he found Blind James Campbell and his band on the streets of Nashville, where they had been a fixture since before World War II. Strachwitz had been given the address by another blues enthusiast. Not strictly blues, the Campbell repertoire spanned a wide range of material beyond blues, mixing old standards, gospel, and country music in the blend. In October 1962, he recorded Campbell and his band in Campbell's living room on a single condenser microphone, Campbell standing directly beneath the mic, his band stationed around him in a circle.

Driving around the South by himself, Strachwitz held more sessions in Macon, Georgia; Birmingham, Alabama; and elsewhere. In Atlanta, he caught one of his all-time favorites, Piano Red, at the Magnolia Ballroom. His raunchy 1951 record of "Red's Boogie" and "Rockin' with Red" was a special favorite of Strachwitz's, although he didn't love the piano man's current rhythm and blues incarnation as Dr. Feelgood and the Interns. In Baton Rouge, he inquired about a preacher he had seen singing on the street with his children the year before and was told that Reverend Overstreet had moved to Phoenix. Passing through Phoenix on his way back to the West Coast, Strachwitz lucked into the reverend's church after stopping for directions at a gas station. He returned to make an album with him and his family in December. He was settling into his calling.

Strachwitz finally made his album with Lightnin' in November 1961 at Sierra Sound Studio in Berkeley, where he had recorded Mercy Dee. Aiming to evoke the sound he loved from the records Lightnin' did on the Herald label in 1954, the last records Lightnin' made before disappearing for several years, he cut Lightnin' on electric guitar, backed solely by bass and drums. Strachwitz acquired the services of the rhythm section from Oakland bluesman Jimmy McCracklin's band. He also recorded Lightnin' on piano, catching him ad-libbing a wonderful, long, rambling blues about the recent fires in Los Angeles. He caught the brooding "California Showers" on his crappy Roberts recorder one rainy afternoon at Lightnin's cousin's house in Oakland, and to complete the album, Lightnin' sent him a couple more songs that he recorded on his own in Houston shortly thereafter.

The subsequent Arhoolie album, *Lightnin' Sam Hopkins* (Arhoolie 1011), occasioned a rift with Mack McCormick in Texas, who could be a gruff and surly character. McCormick was under the impression that he held exclusive recording rights with Lightnin' Hopkins and had been turning out a slew of indifferent albums for the Prestige label in New York. Strachwitz knew better than to think Lightnin' would recognize anyone's exclusive province over him. Lightnin's attitude toward him was changing. They had spent enough time together to become friends, and to Lightnin', Strachwitz's money was as good as anyone else's. "I wanted that record," said Strachwitz.

FILMING WITH THE GERMANS *(1963)*

IN MARCH 1963, Strachwitz signed up to work as a light operator and sound recorder for a husband-wife German documentary film crew, regardless of his lack of experience doing either. Dietrich Wawzyn and his wife, Anna Maria, had done a well-regarded film about religious practices in India and wanted to train their sights on American traditional music. A mutual friend suggested Strachwitz. They gave him a modest salary and set off across the country after starting in the Bay Area, where they filmed the extravagant Oakland preacher King Louis H. Narcisse at his church, one-man band Jesse "Lone Cat" Fuller in his Oakland home, and bluesman Lowell Fulson at the Blue Mirror in San Francisco's Fillmore district.

They headed off, Strachwitz driving his VW panel truck and the Wawzyns in a Mercedes with a 45 RPM record player mounted under the dashboard. Strachwitz was astonished by the revival tent show they filmed outside Phoenix, the preacher running up and down the aisles, screaming his head off, parishioners falling down and rolling on the floor, speaking in tongues. They filmed Reverend Overstreet and his sons, whom Strachwitz had recorded the previous December, and the Wawzyns gifted the reverend—at his request—with the 45 player. In Gallup, New Mexico, they filmed Native American musicians and caught up with Mance Lipscomb and a few of his grandchildren on his front porch in Navasota, Texas.

In Dallas, they got Black Ace in his living room and Alex Moore at the same piano teacher's house where Strachwitz first recorded him. In Houston, they caught Lightnin' Hopkins playing on the street in his neighborhood and steel guitarist Hop Wilson at Irene's. From there, they went to Lake Charles, Louisiana, where record producer Eddie Shuler arranged for them to film accordionist Shorty LeBlanc playing his hit single, "Sugar Bee."

They met folklorist Harry Oster in Baton Rouge, and he took them to the banks of the Mississippi River to film Willie Thomas and his family. In New Orleans, Allan Jaffe of Preservation Hall helped arrange a session with a quartet. It was a union job and that was all the Wawzyns could afford, but Strachwitz made sure they included his traditional jazz hero, clarinetist George Lewis. They filmed the Hodges Brothers in Mississippi on their way to Nashville, where they shot Blind James Campbell and his Nashville Street Band. They also shot an evening at the Grand Ole Opry and some regulation Nashville country singers to Strachwitz's dismay; these artificial, commercial musicians were practically the antithesis of the authentic American music Strachwitz had been showing them.

The Wawzyns followed Strachwitz to Concord, North Carolina, to film J. E. Mainer's Mountaineers. The year before, Strachwitz had been amused visiting Mainer, who had been playing music in North Carolina since before his 1933 radio broadcast debut, when the cagey fiddler coaxed five bucks out of Strachwitz for an interview, along with an additional five bucks for a photograph, eventually sending Strachwitz down the road to a bootlegger to fetch a bottle of white lightning. The previous year, he had been reluctant to record because he hadn't played music in some time, but he had taken the time to practice in the interim and he and his family made an album with Strachwitz while the Wawzyns filmed.

The Wawzyns and Strachwitz parted company in April on the East Coast, but on his way back, Strachwitz found himself driving through Hackberry, Louisiana, which brought to his mind the Hackberry Ramblers, one of the great Cajun string bands of the '30s. The group's 1935 recording of "Jole Blon" was a Cajun classic. He stopped in the town's café and asked the waitress if she knew anything about the group. Indeed, she did. She directed him to the home of the group's founding fiddler, Luderin Darbone, telling Strachwitz to drive out of town on Main Street and turn right on Darbone Street. "You can't miss it," she said.

Without his realizing it, the America that Strachwitz was traveling through was already vanishing. The musicians he recorded from those pre-war recordings—the hillbillies and the blues singers—were nearing senior citizenship, most still at the peak of their powers and commanding their music from a vantage point of age and experience, but not for much longer. Jim Crow laws were only begrudgingly evaporating from the South, and the rediscovery of this music as a treasure of American folklore was years away. Modern life was erasing these pockets of regional culture, as the kind of life that produced this rich tapestry of music was giving way to something they called progress.

In July 1963, Mance Lipscomb returned to the Berkeley Folk Festival, where he traded songs with Pete Seeger at a campfire concert, sat in with hillbilly fiddler J. E. Mainer, and captivated the capacity crowd at the Jubilee Concert in the cavernous Greek Theatre. He was getting to be an old hand at this folk scene. Strachwitz headed back south after the folk festival in his new Volkswagen van, taking Mance home and scouting for old records and new musicians to record. He bought so many records that he burned out his car engine carrying such a heavy load of old shellac 78s.

Having grown up in Europe, Strachwitz could be innocent about racial issues, something circumstances would remind him of occasionally on his travels through the South. Stopping at a West Texas café with Lipscomb, they took seats at the counter and Strachwitz excused himself to go to the bathroom. When he returned, Lipscomb was missing. He asked the counterman where his friend went and was directed to the kitchen, where he found Lipscomb seated. "Chris, this is where I have to go when I eat at white peoples' place," he told Strachwitz.

Strachwitz also experienced the difference between accommodations for the races when he dropped Lipscomb off to stay with some friends in Abilene, Texas, and, too tired to drive to the white section of town, checked into a rundown Black motel so filthy he slept on top of the bedcovers. He was beginning to see America from its dark underside.

In November 1963, Mississippi Delta bluesman Bukka White played a weeklong engagement at Berkeley's Cabale, and Strachwitz was fascinated by his lengthy improvisations and piercing bottleneck guitar playing. Bukka White had a long and distinguished history in the music; he was the first bluesman that his cousin B. B. King ever saw. White traced his music back to Delta blues pioneer Charley Patton and cut a handful of blues classics in the '30s with Memphis Minnie on background vocals. Library of Congress folklorist John Lomax recorded White while he was serving time for assault in Mississippi State Penitentiary (the fearsome Parchman Farm), and he had long been out of the music field when he was rediscovered in 1963 by guitarist John Fahey. Aware of White's song "Aberdeen, Mississippi Blues," Fahey had simply sent a postcard to White addressed to "General Delivery, Aberdeen, Mississippi" and it was forwarded to White where he was living in Memphis.

Strachwitz sat down the Delta blues veteran in his upstairs apartment on Addison Street in Berkeley one afternoon that week and captured his extraordinary, lengthy, unedited improvised blues, some running ten minutes in length, for an Arhoolie album titled *Sky Songs*, because that's where White said he got them. Strachwitz caught them.

The Blues Go to Europe *(1964)*

HORST LIPPMANN and his partner, Fritz Rau, started the American Folk Blues Festival tour in 1962 after contacting Chicago blues kingpin Willie Dixon about arranging the acts to perform. Two years later, while setting up the 1964 tour, they faced a crucial French promoter reluctant to book the show unless Lightnin' Hopkins was on the bill. Lightnin' didn't like to fly. Europe was a long way from Houston. Lippmann reached out to Strachwitz to help convince Lightnin' to make the trip. They agreed to meet in Houston in February 1964 and talk with the recalcitrant bluesman. Strachwitz didn't initially expect much from this winter excursion, but it would prove to be one of his greatest expeditions.

Lippmann was a key figure in the German jazz scene. He played drums during the war in the illegal Frankfurt Hot Club and wrote for the first German jazz magazine. By the mid-'50s, he had partnered with Rau and they produced jazz festivals and promoted concert tours. Along with broadcaster Joachim-Ernst Berendt, they arranged to have the American Folk Blues Festival performances broadcast in Germany, which helped underwrite the enterprise.

These tours proved to be pivotal events in the history of the blues. The entire next generation of British musicians attended shows: Mick Jagger, Keith Richards, Jimmy Page, Robert Plant, Eric Burdon, Eric Clapton, and Stevie Winwood, among others. Most of the acts had never appeared outside the United States and were only slightly known at home. Europeans embraced the musicians and their music like they had never been before. These annual October tours were sparks that not only ignited the spread of blues but established the entire concept of blues festivals.

Strachwitz arrived in Houston a few days ahead of Lippmann and spent his time hanging out with Lightnin', who took Strachwitz in his Cadillac to see his "cousin" Clifton Chenier. Strachwitz knew Chenier from the rock and roll–flavored 45s Chenier did for the Specialty label in the '50s and was not especially enthusiastic at the prospect. They showed up at some tiny beer joint with a low ceiling in Frenchtown on the southeast side of town, where Strachwitz laid his eyes on this scrawny Black man wearing a giant piano accordion, backed only by a drummer bashing away, Chenier wailing away on vocals in some strange French patois that Strachwitz could not under-stand. He was blown away. He had never heard such sounds.

On the break, Chenier came over to greet Hopkins. They were well known to each other. One of Lightnin's wives was a cousin of Chenier's—hence Lightnin' calling him "cousin"—and Lightnin' often used Chenier's brother Cleveland on rubboard around local clubs. Chenier quickly made the tall, smiling white man with the funny accent that Lightnin' introduced to him. "Oh, you a record man," Chenier said. "Let's make a record."

Strachwitz booked a session on February 8, 1964—the day before the Beatles first appeared on *The Ed Sullivan Show*—at Bill Quinn's Gold Star Studios, where Lightnin' made all his records, and despite Strachwitz telling Chenier that he only wanted him and the drummer, Chenier showed up with a full band. He was a veteran of the bayou blues scene and knew the only sound his people wanted was loud, danceable swamp rock blasting from the jukebox. Strachwitz was hardly brokenhearted when Chenier's guitarist blew up his rig—smoke coming out of the amplifier, the works—and Chenier was forced to proceed with only drums and piano. Strachwitz released the results on a 45 RPM single, rare for Arhoolie, but that was what Chenier wanted. Strachwitz enthusiastically laid plans to return and record an album with Chenier at his earliest opportunity.

After meeting with Lippmann and convincing a reluctant Lightnin' to join the European tour that fall—his only condition was that Strachwitz accompany him—Strachwitz left Houston for Mississippi, on his way to yet another incredible discovery. Strachwitz first heard Fred McDowell on field recordings made by Alan Lomax (on the same trip that Lomax recorded hillbilly fiddler J. E. Mainer). He had spent most of his life making his living hardscrabble farming and playing for free at dances and parties on the weekends. When Lomax recorded him in 1959, McDowell had never heard himself before. Five years later, spurred by the song "Write Me a Few Lines," which Lomax had recorded, Strachwitz arrived in Como, Mississippi, with an address supplied by Lomax. He stopped at the local post office to get directions, and when he pulled up at the farm, he saw McDowell getting off a tractor. That evening, in McDowell's living room, he captured the first Arhoolie album by Fred McDowell on the ungainly Magnecord tape machine that replaced his crappy Japanese model, including a new version of "Write Me a Few Lines" and a blistering "Shake 'Em On Down" that would be copied by numerous English rock bands.

On returning to Houston, Strachwitz heard that Lightnin's brother John Henry was out of prison and suggested recording all three brothers together. Lightnin' had boasted of his brothers' skills, and Joel Hopkins had spent time in his youth with Blind Lemon Jefferson. Strachwitz took Joel in his car, Lightnin' packed their mom into his Cadillac, and they made the two-hundred-mile trip to Waxahatchie. The session did not go as planned. All three brothers got drunk. Lightnin', who could be mean when he wanted, got into it with his brother John Henry, and the whole session turned out to be something of a mess, far from the convivial collaboration Strachwitz had envisioned. He went back to Berkeley disappointed in the Hopkins brothers session, but he knew what he had with Fred McDowell and was anxious to get back to Houston and make an entire album with Clifton Chenier.

In October, Strachwitz and Lightnin' flew to Europe on an Air India flight with a connection in New York. When they arrived in Germany, Strachwitz took to his hotel bed, suffering from some mysterious illness that no doctor could diagnose. After a few days of rest and care, he recovered from what may have been something like a nervous breakdown.

The first two tours had greatly expanded the blues community in Great Britain. Howlin' Wolf's "Smokestack Lightnin'" had made a modest appearance on the British pop charts in June, and the charismatic Chicago bluesman was the logical choice for this year's headliner. Sonny Boy Williamson returned from the previous year's tour, this

HUNTING RECORDS
1971, Mamou, Louisiana

Chris never lost his enthusiasm for searching out old 78s on his travels.

time outfitted in full British sartorial splendor of a bowler hat and walking stick. Along with Lightnin', the bill also included Sleepy John Estes and Hammie Nixon, Sunnyland Slim, and others. Sugar Pie DeSanto replaced Mae Mercer midway through the tour. The house band consisted of Willie Dixon on bass alongside guitarist Hubert Sumlin and drummer Clifton James from Wolf's band.

Lightnin' closed the first half of the concerts and left such an impression on the *Melody Maker* reviewer in London that he invoked pioneering blues deity Big Bill Broonzy. He was in top form, and the entire tour had considerable impact on the British music scene, which was at the time only beginning to seep out of art schools. The music was hard to find over there. Willie Dixon would make tapes of his songs for young British musicians. He left a tape for pianist Long John Baldry at the National Jazz Federation that somehow wound up in the hands of the Yardbirds. A few weeks after the tour ended, the Rolling Stones released their version of Howlin' Wolf's "Little Red Rooster," which Dixon wrote, and it sprinted to number one on the charts. In England, the blues revival was on.

Recording the Blues (1965-1966)

WITH ARHOOLIE RECORDS not making enough money to support him, Strachwitz turned to concert promoting with the Berkeley Blues Festival in February 1965 at the Berkeley Community Theater, starring Chuck Berry. He had dabbled in the field with a small Lightnin' Hopkins show a couple of years before, but this was a full program also featuring Big Mama Thornton, the Chambers Brothers, Fred McDowell, and Long Gone Miles, Lightnin's friend from Houston recently relocated to Los Angeles. The father of rock and roll may have seemed like an unlikely headliner for Strachwitz's festival, but Strachwitz loved Chuck Berry's music.

Although Berry masked his rock and roll songs in lightly disguised cynical, smirking condescension, his sound was solidly blues based, and his pianist Johnnie Johnson, who played such a prominent role in his music, was straight out of the Meade Lux Lewis/Albert Ammons boogie-woogie school. Willie Dixon frequently played bass on the sessions. Strachwitz was able to sense the genuine qualities of Chuck Berry, who amused him no end with his businesslike demeanor at the show, demanding to be paid in full in cash before going on. With all his responsibilities as concert producer, Strachwitz did not photograph the event, but he did make some money.

In April 1965, Strachwitz was accompanying Mance Lipscomb on his first East Coast dates at folk clubs and was sitting in the audience at a performance by Mance and Son House in a Georgetown nightclub when forty-one-year-old John Jackson emerged from the crowd to play two numbers. Jackson learned guitar and banjo as a youth growing up in backwoods Virginia and had played in country bands around the region in the early '40s, but he had long given up music. He worked many jobs, including gravedigger. He was accidentally discovered by a Washington folk fan who happened to hear Jackson goofing around on guitar at a gas station. The same fan had brought Jackson to the club to see the other bluesmen. Strachwitz immediately announced he wanted to make a record with Jackson.

He went to Jackson's Fairfax, Virginia, home the next day and recorded Jackson from eleven in the morning until eleven at night, catching an astonishing ninety songs. After his debut album on Arhoolie was released shortly thereafter, Jackson returned to performing music and never dug another grave.

Strachwitz drove Mance back to Navasota and went on to Houston, where he took Clifton Chenier into Bill Quinn's Gold Star Studios and cut his first Arhoolie album in one day. Strachwitz compromised with Chenier on the album, devoting one side to the full band R & B–style tracks Chenier insisted on recording and the other side only Clifton singing in Creole French, his brother on rubboard, and a drummer, for the more primal sound Strachwitz wanted. One song stood out— "Tu les Jours C'est Pas la Meme Chose"—which Strachwitz astutely judged too difficult a title for disc jockeys and changed it to "Louisiana Blues."

The record ignited Chenier's career, not only in the Houston area but throughout Louisiana. The track restored his Creole pride, and he began getting calls for dances at church halls all over Louisiana. He was suddenly the first zydeco star, although Chenier always harbored larger ambitions. He saw himself on the level of a Ray Charles or Fats Domino. Without Strachwitz, he could have easily spent the rest of his life laboring in obscurity. The Arhoolie album *Louisiana Blues and Zydeco* would introduce this spicy and delectable regional delight to a worldwide audience.

Strachwitz traveled on to Helena, Arkansas, intent on meeting with Sonny Boy Williamson to arrange to re-release his early recordings for the tiny Jackson, Mississippi, label Trumpet Records, where Sonny Boy recorded from 1951 until the company went bankrupt three years later. Strachwitz had been putting out a series of historic recordings, largely drawn from his own encyclopedic 78 RPM record collection, on his Blues Classics label, and he knew the great bluesman from touring Europe together. He signed a deal with Sonny Boy, although the label owner would later sue Strachwitz, leading to him settling the lawsuit by buying the masters.

He accompanied Sonny Boy to the radio station KFFA for his daily, fifteen-minute radio broadcast. He hung his microphone next to the one the station used and recorded the show from inside the booth. The announcer can be heard in the background. After the radio show, Strachwitz took Sonny Boy and his two accompanists outside the radio station and posed them for photographs in the alley.

Strachwitz also found time on this trip to swing through Como, Mississippi, and record much of a second Arhoolie album by Fred McDowell. He would finish it in July in the living room of his new home in the Berkeley hills when McDowell came to appear at the annual Berkeley Folk Festival, alongside such folk music notables as Mike Seeger of the New Lost City Ramblers, Sam Hinton, Jean Ritchie, and Tom Paxton. Strachwitz had also arranged for an appearance by Cajun string band Hackberry Ramblers, but gentle, warm McDowell was the darling of the weekend.

Around Berkeley, the folk scene encompassed the country blues world. Old-timers such as Reverend Gary Davis, Jesse Fuller, Big Joe Williams, and others mingled with earnest young collegiate musicians raised on Kingston Trio and Joan Baez records. Strachwitz recorded a few examples, including a full-length album with singer-songwriter Alice Stuart and a collection of Berkeley folkies, *Out West: Berkeley*. In October 1965, a group of itinerant nouveau jug band musicians from the Berkeley folk scene who had recently changed their name to Country Joe and the Fish came to Strachwitz's living room to record a couple of songs for a talking magazine—a pamphlet packaged with a record—the group planned to distribute in time for a big Vietnam War protest. Their manager arranged for Strachwitz to record the song, which he agreed to publish in exchange for his fee for the recording. The song, "I-Feel-Like-I'm-Fixin'-to-Die Rag," would eventually appear on three-million-selling albums after Country Joe McDonald made the song famous with his solo performance at the Woodstock festival.

He left for England and the next American Folk Blues Festival tour with Fred McDowell later the same month, part of an all-star cast that included Big Mama Thornton, Buddy Guy, John Lee Hooker, and J. B. Lenoir. Strachwitz took the stellar Chicago blues rhythm section along with guitar great Buddy Guy into Wessex Studio, a converted church in Highbury Park, London, for a daylong session backing Big Mama Thornton, whom he first saw play at a Santa Cruz beach bar playing drums and singing in 1961. He had recommended her to the Monterey Jazz Festival in 1964, where she was the surprise hit of the blues afternoon. Strachwitz told promoter Horst Lippmann about her, and after overcoming her reluctance to fly, she came on the tour and was blowing away crowds at every stop. The session was more party than work. Strachwitz even paired Big Mama with Fred McDowell for a couple of extraordinary collaborations.

Back in Berkeley, Strachwitz consulted with the German producers Lippmann and Rau on a country music festival modeled after their American Folk Blues Festival tours featuring the New Lost City Ramblers, Roscoe Holcomb, the Stanley Brothers, and others who did not prove to be as successful as the blues tours. He spotted another future bluegrass star when he presented a concert by Bill Monroe and his Blue Grass Boys in December at a local junior high school auditorium. Monroe's guitarist Del McCoury sang a song, "I Wonder Where You Are Tonight," that hit Strachwitz so hard he would seek out McCoury two years later and initiate his solo career just to record a version of that song.

In April 1966, he continued his promotion work with the second annual Berkeley Blues Festival, in association with UC Berkeley, at Harmon Gym on the campus. Not only did the lineup feature the stars of Arhoolie—Lightnin' Hopkins, Mance Lipscomb, and Clifton Chenier—but the Muddy Waters band with James Cotton on harmonica and Otis Spann on piano. While Strachwitz drove the great blues pianist across the bay from San Francisco, Spann asked Strachwitz to make a record with him, but Strachwitz couldn't see how he could improve on the album Spann made with Nat Hentoff for the Candid label. Again, Strachwitz was too busy to take photographs or record the event. When he later heard the tape of the broadcast by the campus radio station, he did make an album of the live recordings. But, as long as they were in town, he did also record Mance in his living room and took Big Mama Thornton into Wally Heider Studios in San Francisco with the Muddy Waters band.

Cajuns and Austrians (1967)

IN APRIL 1966, Strachwitz left for his annual southern sojourn. On this trip to Texas, he spent some time skulking around San Antonio, investigating the Mexican American music scene. Strachwitz first fell in love with the sounds of Mexican ranchera music on the radio as a youth when he was attending the Cate School and later, while going to college in Pomona, from a jukebox in a bar he frequented. He thought it sounded like country music, only sung in Spanish. He met with Texas record labels that specialized in the music, sought out old 78s, and contacted accordionist Narciso Martínez, widely considered the father of the Tex-Mex conjunto sound, but he didn't seriously consider recording these musicians because he thought that the little regional labels had the scene covered.

In Houston, he caught Joe Patek and his Czech Bohemian band, music he learned to love from Texas radio. He held sessions with a middling Texas blues guitarist named Larry O. Williams and the next day he cut the second Arhoolie album by Clifton Chenier. They brought in fiddler Morris Chenier, Clifton's uncle, who broke the bridge holding his

RECORDING AT HOME
1960, BERKELEY, CALIFORNIA

Chris and his reel-to-reel recorder in his Berkeley hills home (with dog).

strings while recording, which gave his solo an accidentally fabulous out-of-tune sound on the track "Black Gal," which unexpectedly wound up a regional favorite.

Strachwitz bounced through Shreveport to Mamou, Louisiana, where he recorded Cajun harmonica player Isom Fontenot in one of the other musicians' houses. He met with one of the few people who dealt in this kind of music, record producer J. D. Miller, in Lake Charles, Louisiana, but Miller played cagey about sharing his contacts and Strachwitz went on his own to Basile, Louisiana, to find one of the great original Cajun musicians.

Accordionist Nathan Abshire recorded back as far as the '30s but made an amazing comeback after World War II. After the war, he settled in Basile, Louisiana, where he performed regularly at the Avalon Club. He released his best-known record, "Pine Grove Blues," in 1949 and recorded prolifically for a variety of regional labels throughout the '50s and '60s. Strachwitz easily recognized his familiarity with the Black blues idiom in his signature piece. Abshire was a lonesome, genial character who grew up in the far reaches of the bayous and never learned to read or write. Strachwitz cut Abshire with Dewey and Rodney Balfa—veteran Cajun recording artists themselves—in the back room of the Frontier Bar in downtown Basile. Two days later, he was in New Orleans interviewing jazz guitarist Danny Barker. From there, he headed north to Memphis, Nashville, and New York City.

Back in San Francisco, the blues had exploded on the acid-rock ballroom circuit. Alongside hippie rock bands like Jefferson Airplane, Grateful Dead, Quicksilver Messenger Service, and others, authentic blues players shared the bill. B. B. King, Muddy Waters, Howlin' Wolf, Otis Rush, Junior Wells, even Lightnin' all played the Fillmore and Avalon Ballrooms. Strachwitz recorded Big Mama Thornton live at the Fillmore Auditorium in October 1966, although he didn't catch anything he liked that much. But the blues renaissance was a big part of what was going on in San Francisco, which was turning into a freewheeling musical laboratory, and even Strachwitz wasn't immune to the spirit of experimentation suddenly in the air.

Earlier that year, in January 1966, a German friend had dragged an unsuspecting Strachwitz to see a double bill of the John Coltrane Quartet and Thelonious Monk Quartet at the Jazz Workshop in San Francisco. Strachwitz, who had no interest in any jazz styles past the swing era, happened to catch Coltrane at a brief transitional moment in his career when he not only added his wife, Alice Coltrane, and saxophonist Pharoah Sanders to the band, but matched drummer Elvin Jones with second drummer Rashied Ali. Strachwitz was thunderstruck by the powerful twin drummers who trained their ferocious beats at him like laser beams in the tiny club (he subsequently walked out on Monk). He immediately developed an unlikely interest in modern jazz. He spotted guitarist Jerry Hahn in the John Handy Quintet, and in April 1967, just before leaving on his southern trip, he took Hahn and Handy bandmate violinist Michael White into Sierra Sound in Berkeley for two days of hard-blowing free jazz, a first for Arhoolie (even though the album was released under a different label at first, Changes).

The Summer of Love was approaching—hippies were swarming over Berkeley—and even Strachwitz couldn't resist the pull of the flower children. The day before the Hahn sessions, he went into Sierra Sound with a Berkeley psychedelic rock band called Notes from the Underground, who switched off weekends with Country Joe and the Fish at the Jabberwock. A subsequent EP, also released on Changes, led to the group signing with Vanguard Records, where their debut album sank without a trace.

But the big event for the year would be a six-week trip to Austria, where Austrian blues collector Johnny Parth, who Strachwitz met in Munich on the 1964 American Folk Blues Festival tour with Lightnin', wanted him to record authentic Austrian folk music. Strachwitz learned to love yodeling while he was first in Austria when he was in the army, but Parth wanted nothing to do with anything that commercial. In some ways, the trip represented a return to Strachwitz's roots in Germany and there were plenty of relatives to visit, but Parth was intent on capturing genuine Austrian folk music—the way Strachwitz recorded the blues in America.

He dragged Strachwitz to the top of a mountain, bearing a bottle of wine as a gift, to record an old married couple, Fefi and Josef Eibisberger, singing the old songs in a field surrounded by goats. Parth was especially enthusiastic about the woman's work on the hackbrett—hammered dulcimer—and Strachwitz had unwittingly captured a rare and precious piece of Austrian folklore. They recorded one gentleman who played a marimba made of bricks. They caught an organist on the streets of Vienna. They captured three farmers singing Gstanzls—risqué traditional folk songs. They recorded a brass band on his new Sennheiser microphone and Uher tape recorder.

Strachwitz's records were getting around, even if record sales still couldn't fully support him. Despite the small sales numbers, discerning ears were hearing what he was doing. In October, while in Los Angeles holding sessions with Clifton Chenier, Strachwitz met with Jerry Wexler of Atlantic Records, who was interested in signing Chenier. Strachwitz was amenable to seeing Chenier on a major label, but they couldn't come to terms.

In December, hoping to avoid the Christmas madness, Strachwitz headed out again. He went to Chicago to do a second session with mandolinist Johnny Young (the previous year's session had been produced by Pete Welding). Young was a struggling, old-time blues musician living in desperate poverty. He played more old-fashioned, more country-style blues than most of the Chicago guys and, consequently, didn't get a lot of work. To co-produce the session, Strachwitz brought his associate from the American Folk Blues Festival tours, Willie Dixon, a Chicago blues cornerstone, who added genius harmonica player Walter "Shakey" Horton; guitarist Jimmy Dawkins; and Howlin' Wolf's pianist, Lafayette Leake, to the date, as Strachwitz started to get his feet wet in the once-thriving world of Chicago blues.

In New York City, he visited with John Cohen of the New Lost City Ramblers and auditioned the Sun Ra Arkestra at the Folklore Center. After a week in New York, he went to Virginia to record a second album with John Jackson, and the next day, he was in York, Pennsylvania, conducting the first solo sessions by Del McCoury, Bill Monroe's former guitarist who Strachwitz saw sing two years before in Berkeley. McCoury was out of the music business, working in logging, but he was game to record with Strachwitz.

In Atlanta, he called boogie-woogie master Piano Red. In Memphis, he looked around for blues singer Bobo Jenkins. He visited Cajun record producer Floyd Soileau of Swallow Records at the company headquarters in Ville Platt, Louisiana. In New Orleans, he met with blind bluesman Snooks Eaglin. He saw country music great Ernest Tubb perform in New Braunsfel, Texas. In Houston, he started an album at ACA Studios with Juke Boy Bonner, a guitarist and rack harmonica player in the mold of Jimmy Reed, who wrote poems that were published in the newspaper. He returned to Berkeley on Christmas Day.

MEMPHIS BLUES AGAIN (1968)

IN 1968, for the first time since he started, Strachwitz did not make a trip down south, outside of a quick outing in January to Houston to record Juke Boy Bonner. He hired Barrett Hansen—best known as novelty record disc jockey Dr. Demento—to oversee sessions in Los Angeles with Big Mama Thornton (where Strachwitz finally got her to record "Ball and Chain," her song that Janis Joplin of hippie rock band Big Brother and the Holding Company was making famous) and her guitarist Bee Houston, who also turned in a quietly excellent solo set for Arhoolie.

In November 1968, Strachwitz returned to Chicago, where he held three sessions with the remarkable Earl Hooker, who had languished like buried treasure in Chicago blues clubs. Buddy Guy had recommended Earl Hooker when Strachwitz asked the guitarist who he should record in Chicago. Growing up there, Hooker played guitar on the streets with his childhood friend Bo Diddley. He recorded extensively through the '50s (including the original version of the B. B. King hit "Sweet Little Angel") and partnered productively with harmonica player Junior Wells for several years. But Hooker, who had suffered from tuberculosis since he was a kid, was in and out of hospitals his whole life. He had only recently left a yearlong stay, put together a new band against doctor's advice, and was back in the clubs when Strachwitz approached him about recording. The title track to the album, "Two Bugs and a Roach," was a tour de force, talking blues about being in the hospital. He would be dead in eighteen months.

Strachwitz also joined forces again with Willie Dixon to produce a big session with guitarist John Littlejohn, a full band including two horns. Littlejohn frustrated Strachwitz's efforts to have him play slide guitar in the Elmore James style—Littlejohn wanted to croon Brook Benton pop songs—and they went through countless tries to get James's "Dust My Broom," although most of the rest of the tracks from the session were first takes.

He headed down to Texas to cut Juke Boy Bonner at ACA Studios in Houston, taped Mance Lipscomb with a relative playing bass and a drummer in Navasota, and, in San Antonio, he recorded George Coleman, known as Bongo Joe, a street musician who played a specially modified fifty-five-gallon oil drum, the kind of American music eccentric that only Strachwitz would notice. He wanted to record Bongo Joe on the bridge where he customarily performed, but the cord for his recorder wouldn't reach, so they went to Strachwitz's friend Larry Skoog's house and recorded the album there.

Back in Berkeley, he continued his flirtation with modern jazz, cutting albums with free jazz saxist Sonny Simmons and a larger session with drummer Smiley Winters. Strachwitz mistitled "Seven Dances of Salome" as "Seven Dances of Salami" on the Simmons album and mistook the Coltrane tribute "To Trane" for "Two Trains" on the Winters album. He was still too down home for modern jazz.

But blues had broken into the contemporary music scene. With British blues-rock bands like Cream, Savoy Brown, Fleetwood Mac, and others, and underground American rock bands adopting electric blues as part of their repertoires, the record industry suddenly saw blues on the menu. Strachwitz was commissioned to produce an album by Lightnin' Hopkins for the Poppy label, a messy session with a band backing up Lightnin' on a set of old favorites from his repertoire. Blue Thumb Records, a hip boutique label out of Beverly Hills, hired Strachwitz to make a record at the fourth annual Memphis Country Blues Festival in June 1969 (they also licensed an album's worth of Clifton Chenier tracks from his Arhoolie catalog).

While the festival stage at the Overton Park Shell mixed homegrown soul by Rufus Thomas and the Bar-Kays with visiting firemen like Texas newcomer Johnny Winter, the bill also featured almost one dozen authentic old bluesmen, ranging in age from fifty-eight-year-old Bukka White to Nathan Beauregard, who pleaded guilty to ninety-five, although many suspected he was even older.

These tribal elders sat backstage in their starched white shirts in the sweltering Memphis summer sun waiting to be called onstage. The concert ran without a schedule, and nobody knew who would play next, so the bluesmen waited patiently, some drinking more than was prudent. A television crew filmed all weekend for a PBS-TV special.

**CHRIS WITH FRED MCDOWELL
1971, COMO, MISSISSIPPI**

Chris recorded extensively
with Fred McDowell, one of the
last great Mississippi country
bluesmen, and took him to Europe
on the American Folk Blues
Festival tour.

Strachwitz booked time at local studios and cut Bukka White, Nathan Beauregard, Sleepy John Estes, Fred McDowell (with harmonica player Johnny Woods), fife and drum music with Napoleon Strickland and Otha Turner, and Memphis's own Furry Lewis. Guitarist John Fahey was around helping. Blue Thumb released a double-record set of the recordings, although after seeing that royalties were not forthcoming, Strachwitz appropriated the tapes for Arhoolie.

In July, he was back in Berkeley taking Earl Hooker into Berkeley's Sierra Sound with a red-hot band of local blues-rockers and cutting Fred McDowell in his living room with a young white protégé that McDowell discovered in Portland, Oregon, named Mike Russo (and bassist John Kahn, later long-standing member of Jerry Garcia solo bands). The blues was spreading beyond the music's native habitat.

In October, Strachwitz again accompanied the American Folk Blues Festival tour around Europe on a program largely assembled by Strachwitz on behalf of Lippmann and Rau. He booked Arhoolie artists Clifton Chenier, John Jackson, Earl Hooker, Alex Moore, and Juke Boy Bonner. For the first time, Willie Dixon was not involved, but the program was rounded out by the Chicago blues stalwarts guitarist Magic Sam and harmonica player Carey Bell. In Stuttgart, Germany, Strachwitz squeezed in a quick studio session with Alex Moore and John Jackson. He flew straight back from Europe to Houston, where he conducted sessions with Clifton Chenier at Bill Quinn's Gold Star Studios.

Returning to Berkeley, in November he recorded a wealth of Mance Lipscomb songs at Sierra Sound and another album with Lightnin' in his Berkeley hills living room, including Lightnin's tribute to Berkeley hippies, "Up on Telegraph Avenue." A week later, Strachwitz held sessions in his living room with Big Joe Williams, accompanied by young harmonica ace Charlie Musselwhite, who was known as "Memphis Charlie" when he arrived on the Chicago blues scene where he and Big Joe first met. The two old friends broke the blues glass ceiling on Chicago's Old Town, far across the city from the blues clubs on the city's South and West Sides, when they started appearing together at Big John's on North Wells Street, where the Paul Butterfield Blues Band subsequently took over as the house band. Musselwhite relocated to the Bay Area after his first album was released on Vanguard Records and had been doing some part-time work on the loading dock for Arhoolie.

Corridos and Conjuntos (1970)

STRACHWITZ did not plan on recording Los Pingüinos del Norte, the conjunto he was going to see in a cantina across the river in Piedras Negras, Mexico. As much as he loved the corridos and rancheras, he never seriously considered recording the music. Not knowing what to expect, he and his two associates, Jerry Abrams and Rumel Fuentes, entered the dingy border town bar on a dusty afternoon in May 1970. He did not figure on being swept up in a maelstrom of sound, music, and excitement that would prove to be a major pivot point in his life in music.

The men in the audience shouted out gritos—exclamations of approval—with the fervor of amens at a Baptist church. No women were allowed in the cantina, and Strachwitz was overwhelmed by the machismo of the scene. He knew instantly that he wanted to record this music live to try to capture this raucous atmosphere. He went to the car, where he kept his seventy-pound Magnecord tape recorder in the trunk, and lugged it back to the bar, only to have the owner tell them he didn't want them to record there—it would bother his patrons. They quickly located another bar down the street, and Strachwitz made his first Tex-Mex album that afternoon.

This trip south had started immediately after Strachwitz attended the first New Orleans Jazz and Heritage Festival with a rollicking swamp blues session the next day, April 27, in Baton Rouge, Louisiana, with Excello Records veterans Silas Hogan, Arthur "Guitar" Kelly, Whispering Smith, and Howlin' Wolf's old pianist, Henry Gray. He stopped in Houston to cut some tracks with Clifton Chenier at Jones Studio.

It was Berkeley folklorist Archie Green who had recommended Strachwitz look up Texas attorney Jerry Abrams; he represented the farmworkers' union and knew the border scene. In McAllen, Texas, Abrams introduced Strachwitz to activist and musician Rumel Fuentes, who took them across the border to hear Los Pingüinos del Norte.

In Mexico, they called it *música norteño*, or northern music, but in Texas, it was simply known as Tex-Mex, this unique style of Mexican folk music that had grown up along the border and flourished in recordings since the '20s. Music publisher Ralph Peer—shortly after he discovered Jimmie Rodgers and the Carter Family in the same day at auditions in Bristol, Virginia, effectively inventing modern country music in a single stroke—stumbled across the Mexican music in El Paso in 1928 when he was looking for cowboy songs. He found these narrative ballads—corridos—living folk music composed of topical ballads that often went back to the Mexican Revolution.

During Prohibition, Juárez was a boomtown and the city collected some of the best musicians in Mexico. American record labels like Victor, Bluebird, and Okeh recorded

Spanish-language corridos through the '30s in San Antonio. American record companies recorded extensively in Texas until after World War II, when small regional labels stepped up, South Texas companies such as Ideal, Falcon, Corona, and Rio.

For Strachwitz, it was the blues all over again. No Anglos whatsoever were interested in this music, and the few Latino scholars who studied the music concentrated on the more literary ballad forms. Norteño music was poor people's music, and nobody cared about it but the people who made it and the people who listened to it. The history of the music was not readily available. The old records were difficult to find. The musicians were aging. He felt like he had stepped into a parallel universe.

For ten years, he had plumbed the blues world and the rewards were diminishing. He had scoured the South for any remaining vernacular musicians he could find. He came late to the Chicago blues scene, which had practically dried up and blown away by the time Strachwitz started mining there. He had made every kind of blues record, some many times, and the new blues musicians were all white, devoid of the cultural associations that made the music so attractive to Strachwitz. To him, blues was never a musical idiom; it was a way of life. And just as intriguing as the life of Lightnin' Hopkins was to him, now these Texas-Mexican musicians with their accordions and bajo sextos captivated Strachwitz.

Strachwitz had been a pioneer in a reawakening of interest in American music that was spreading out in different places in different ways. This trip had started at the first New Orleans Jazz and Heritage Festival the last week in April at Congo Square, the historic slave market on the edge of the French Quarter in New Orleans. The festival was a long-overdue recognition of that city's unique and distinctive culture. Promoter George Wein had already established highly successful operations with the Newport Jazz Festival in 1954 and the Newport Folk Festival in 1959. He brought in a couple of students from the Tulane jazz center, Quint Davis and Quint's girlfriend at the time, Allison Miner, who went on to become manager of Professor Longhair and others. She and Davis hunted the Cajun country for offbeat regional music, relying on Strachwitz for advice, as they knew little about the regional music since they were New Orleans people.

It was very traditional, oriented toward both gospel and jazz. Al Hirt and Pete Fountain, fixtures on Bourbon Street, appeared—Fountain inaugurated the festival with a midnight riverboat concert. Clifton Chenier made a rare New Orleans appearance, off his typical crawdad circuit (Strachwitz introduced Chenier at his festival performance). It was a happy, festive affair, attended by only a few hundred people, with gospel queen Mahalia Jackson joining one of the brass bands for an impromptu "Just a Closer Walk with Thee," comedian Woody Allen sitting in on clarinet on a second line with the Olympia Brass Band, and Duke Ellington presiding over the final concert. Regional food and arts and crafts filled the grounds, and many of the people slipped in for free through holes cut in the temporary fence around the festival. From these modest beginnings, one of the world's great music festivals began to grow.

In August, Strachwitz attended the second annual Ann Arbor Blues Festival in Michigan, the first all-blues festival in the country, at the recently renamed Otis Spann Memorial Field. Spann, who had died in April and was buried in an unmarked grave in Chicago, had been scheduled to appear at the festival.

For the second year, the college student promoters, in association with the university, pulled together a historic program that featured a Who's Who of blues—Bobby Bland,

Buddy Guy and Junior Wells, Albert King, T-Bone Walker, Big Joe Turner, Howlin' Wolf and John Lee Hooker, among many others. Arhoolie artists Mance Lipscomb, Fred McDowell, John Jackson, Juke Boy Bonner, and Johnny Young were on the bill. Son House and Robert Pete Williams brought the authentic Mississippi Delta blues, and Texas guitarslinger Johnny Winter represented the new generation of blues musicians. This kind of celebration of the music would have been unthinkable only a few years before, but now blues was on the scene.

You Gotta Move (1971–1972)

WITH COUNTRY JOE'S "I-Feel-Like-I'm-Fixin'-to-Die Rag" a centerpiece to both the movie and soundtrack album from the Woodstock festival, Strachwitz enjoyed a publishing windfall like he had never seen before. He took half of the first check and made a down payment on a building with an upholstery shop in the storefront on San Pablo Avenue in El Cerrito. When the upholstery shop caught fire, Strachwitz took over the entire building and opened a retail record store, Down Home Music. He later added a fireproof vault for his massive 78 record library. He was beginning to build his folk music empire.

The Rolling Stones recorded Fred McDowell's "You Got to Move" on the band's 1971 *Sticky Fingers* album from his second Arhoolie album and credited the song to McDowell, although they neglected to pay royalties. A lawsuit was eventually settled, where McDowell shared the copyright to the traditional song with Reverend Gary Davis, allowing Strachwitz to present McDowell with a generous check before he died, far and away the most money he ever made in music.

In February 1971, Strachwitz made an album with harmonica player Charlie Musselwhite, whose 1966 debut album, *Stand Back!*, was produced by Strachwitz's old friend Sam Charters as a kind of competition with the Paul Butterfield Blues Band. The track "Cristo Redentor" gained a fair amount of airplay on underground radio, and his band was a popular attraction at Bay Area clubs. The album was a rare incursion into the world of white blues by Strachwitz, but Musselwhite quickly outsold all other Arhoolie releases.

Strachwitz started his annual southern trip at the second annual New Orleans Jazz and Heritage Festival, held in Congo Square again and also, again, not that well attended. But Dizzy Gillespie oversaw a tribute to Louis Armstrong, the highlight of which as the first appearance in New Orleans by Armstrong's old bandmate Kid Ory since he left town in 1919. The eighty-four-year-old trombonist was retired and living in Hawaii, but when he trotted out his old warhorse "Muskrat Ramble," he invoked the entire history of New Orleans music. Dizzy Gillespie also found time to sit in briefly with Arhoolie artist Bongo Joe on the festival grounds, banging along on the oil drum with the eccentric street musician.

After New Orleans, Strachwitz recorded old-time Creole guys Bois Sec Ardoin on accordion and Canray Fontenot on fiddle at Ardoin's home near Mamou, Louisiana. Although the duo ventured out to the New Orleans Jazz and Heritage Festival and the Newport Folk Festival, they had been playing for dances and parties most weekends around their neighborhood for the previous thirty-five years and were steeped deep in Creole culture; Ardoin's cousin Amédé Ardoin was the first Black Creole to make records in the '20s. The next day, he cut the great Cajun accordionist Austin Pitre both in his garage and live at the Silver Star, a roadhouse about six miles north of Opelousas, Louisiana. Dissatisfied with his recording levels on the drums, Strachwitz left the recordings unreleased for years. From there, he went to Crawford, Mississippi, where Big Joe Williams lived, and recorded Big Joe and some of the local talent Big Joe found, although nothing Strachwitz was wild about. The blues were coming to an end for him.

He returned to Mississippi to go into Cosimo Matassa's French Quarter studio, where Fats Domino and Little Richard made all their records, to cut the New Orleans Ragtime Orchestra. At that moment in the pop music world, ragtime—or, more specifically, the music of ragtime composer Scott Joplin—was enjoying an unexpected revival thanks to the soundtrack of the popular film *The Sting*. Strachwitz's friend Lars Edegran, a Swede expat living in New Orleans, had discovered some previously unknown written orchestral arrangements from the original ragtime era—before this, musicians could only speculate about the authentic sound of the ragtime orchestra— and he and Strachwitz produced a gently spectacular album that brilliantly evoked a long-gone era.

In October, after recording L. C. Robinson with the Muddy Waters band in August at Wally Heider's in San Francisco, Strachwitz went back for a second trip to Austria with Johnny Parth. The first trip had been relegated to Vienna and the environs, but this time Strachwitz bought a car in London and they covered a far wider territory. In Switzerland, having negotiated a large recent sale of old blues records to a French collector, Strachwitz splurged on a new Nagra portable recorder and a pair of Sennheiser condenser microphones, graduating to stereo for the first time.

In Salzburg, they recorded the yodeler Anna Gratz, although Parth was dismissive of her as not authentic. They found accordionist Christian Ortner with his song "In Heaven There Is No Wine" and trekked to a Styrian mountaintop to catch the Original Herberstein Trio—clarinet, accordion, and hammered dulcimer. They encountered a singing little person who happily posed for photos with the record producers. In Innsbruck, they met more studied, younger folk singers who practiced the old songs. Despite his fluent German, Strachwitz struggled to understand the thick regional dialects in the rural areas they were traveling through.

In January 1972, he took Musselwhite's backup group, the Charles Ford Band, into the studio. These young white blues musicians grew up in the sticks of Ukiah, California, where they first heard the blues by the Paul Butterfield Blues Band. Guitarist Robben Ford, who would go on to have a formidable career playing with George Harrison, Miles Davis, and others, was a phenomenon barely out of his teens. Strachwitz knew them through Musselwhite. For Strachwitz, this qualified as a strictly commercial enterprise, but he couldn't help but appreciate the young musicians' dedication. In February, he recorded Juke Boy Bonner in his living room and chased Mance Lipscomb around several Northern California dates to record him live.

In May, on his annual trip to the South, he finally convinced Piano Red to make a record with him, his boogie-woogie hero since his big 1951 hits, "Red's Boogie" and "Rockin' with Red." He had been disappointed with Red's rhythm and blues band he had seen at the Magnolia Ballroom in Atlanta ten years before, but, by now, Red was playing solo piano for tourists in a vast shopping and entertainment complex called

Underground Atlanta. After some difficulty finding an appropriate piano, Strachwitz eventually caught Red playing solo piano in his own home.

In Austin, Texas, Strachwitz ran some experimental sessions with Rumel Fuentes, the Mexican activist and musician who had introduced him to Los Pingüinos del Norte. Fuentes recorded a bunch of corridos with Strachwitz, but Strachwitz was surprised at how short the songs were. He was interested in the lengthy, more complex storytelling of the older corridos and didn't know what to do with the Fuentes tapes, which remained unreleased for many years. He was only starting to figure out what to do with the Mexican music.

Back in Berkeley, he concentrated on making an album with a promising young Black blues pianist named Dave Alexander. He released an album of old tapes by Memphis one-man band Dr. Ross, whom Strachwitz came to know on the American Folk Blues Festival tours. Strachwitz suspected the forty-five songs he bought from a Memphis collector had been stolen, but he went ahead, put out the record, and paid Dr. Ross.

In November, Strachwitz recorded what could be one of the greatest live albums ever with Clifton Chenier at St. Mark's Hall in Richmond, California. Chenier had played these French dances before at the Catholic church, with a substantial part of its congregation coming from Louisiana. They were joyful, down home affairs with the congregants reliving life back home with an evening of dancing, eating gumbo, drinking, and socializing. Strachwitz hired a portable multitrack recorder and caught an amazing thirty-eight songs. Chenier pumped that forty-five-pound accordion for three and a half hours before taking a break. When he returned for one final hour-long set, he was wearing a crown because he was the King of Zydeco.

CHULAS FRONTERAS *(1975–1976)*

IN 1973, Strachwitz began issuing his series chronicling the history of the music that had begun to consume him, "Texas-Mexican Border Music," the first comprehensive effort at defining the music and collecting the history. He had purchased Harry Oster's label, Folk-Lyric Records, in 1970, and, after reissuing some of Oster's old recordings on the revived label, he started pumping out his Mexican American records on Folk-Lyric.

Since the beginning of Arhoolie, Strachwitz had developed a series of historic reissues for both country blues (Blues Classics) and hillbilly and Cajun music (Old Timey) from his personal 78 collection. He was largely responsible for reviving the interest in the works of figures as significant as Memphis Minnie or Blind Blake, whose music would have been lost without Strachwitz. With norteño music, there was no history. The little labels that made these records paid no attention to the legacy of the music. Norteño had lived in the present tense its whole life, and Strachwitz was among the first record collectors and folklore scholars to even notice the entire field. His reissues were the first serious effort to recount the music's illustrious past. Right from the start, his border music series began to celebrate the work of unsung pioneers such as accordionist Narciso Martínez or vocalist Lydia Mendoza.

His annual southern trip in April 1974 reflected his shifting priorities. He bounced around New Orleans, Eunice, and Lawtell, Louisiana. He made test recordings of some

CHRIS WITH BIG JOE WILLIAMS AND HIS FAMILY
1971, CRAWFORD, MISSISSIPPI

Chris stopped at Big Joe's house to record him one last time, met and was photographed with Joe's extended family.

bluegrass and finished the album that he had started two years before with Bois Sec Ardoin and Canray Fontenot at Ardoin's home in Mamou. In Austin, Texas, he recorded an album with country singer Bill Neely, a fixture on the Austin folk scene since the late '40s and a prototype for Texas singer-songwriters like Guy Clark, Jerry Jeff Walker, and others. Strachwitz was intrigued with his songs like "Satan's Burning Hell," "Black Land Farmer," and "Skid Row," which wound wry social commentary into his honky-tonk numbers, and he cut an album with Neely at his Austin home. He tried some recordings with pianist Robert Shaw, whom Mack McCormick had recorded for Arhoolie in 1963. Shaw was a link to the pre-war Texas barrelhouse piano style with a vast repertoire who Strachwitz felt should be recorded more, although he did not release any of the recordings he made with Shaw on this trip for many years.

In San Antonio, however, Strachwitz recorded Trio San Antonio featuring forty-three-year-old accordionist Fred Zimmerle, a leading figure in the music who brought the traditional duet-style vocals to the accordion-driven instrumental sound of norteño music when he was a young man in the '40s. Trio San Antonio was formed in 1946 and made records, first for RCA Victor, and then with many regional labels in South Texas through the '50s. Although the members always kept their day jobs, they played countless parties, dances, cantinas, and fiestas, keeping the old songs alive on the West Side.

Andrés Berlanga, the sixty-seven-year-old guitarist and vocalist whom Strachwitz recorded with Zimmerle, first started making records in the '30s (including one session in the same hotel on the same day as bluesman Robert Johnson). He spent the Depression playing for tourists in the Plaza, but after the war he took a job with the civil service and quit music until Zimmerle enlisted him in the '50s. Martin Chavarría, sixty-six years old, also on the sessions at the Zimmerle house, recorded extensively through the '30s with his brothers as Los Hermanos Chavarría. Bassist Juan Viesca also went back to the '40s on the San Antonio scene.

In Berkeley, Strachwitz had started a record distributorship to handle European lines and other specialty labels that was keeping him busy and filling the Arhoolie pipeline with more product. The retail record store, Down Home Music, was also doing business, so Strachwitz was finally making a living in the music business. He was also doing less recording, although he did find time to go to Louisiana that October and make what is widely regarded as Clifton Chenier's finest album, *Bogalusa Boogie*, his seventh album for Arhoolie, at the Studio in the Country in Bogalusa, a modern facility opened in 1972 in a twenty-six-acre pine forest about seventy miles north of New Orleans. While Strachwitz credits the studio with setting up the band's equipment in advance so that the musicians could step into the studio and start playing instead of wasting the first hour or so getting ready to record, the engineering staff gave the session a silken sound and a fine mix beyond the typical Arhoolie production. They expertly caught the live sound that Strachwitz liked.

In December, he and filmmaker Les Blank arrived in San Antonio to begin shooting the documentary *Chulas Fronteras*, the film that would, more than any other single thing, galvanize Strachwitz's immersion in the Tex-Mex music world. When he decided to make a documentary about this music, he immediately consulted Blank. He had known Blank since spending time in the '60s at the Los Angeles folk club the Ash Grove and admired his handmade documentaries on Lightnin' Hopkins and Mance Lipscomb, films that Strachwitz had nothing to do with producing. A hulking giant introvert, Blank refused to intrude on filming his subjects by interviewing them. He had in the past used third parties to ask questions off camera, and Strachwitz would serve that role on this film (with the help of an interpreter), which he was financing and would act as both producer and sound recorder.

As much as Strachwitz had studied the records, he knew little of the scene and very few of the musicians and didn't really speak much Spanish. The filming of *Chulas Fronteras*, in many ways, was research-in-action for Strachwitz as he navigated his way through San Antonio's West Side, going to Houston to catch the great Lydia Mendoza, a Tejano star since her first solo recording and 1937 hit, "Mal Hombre," and the Rio Grande Valley, where they sought out the sixty-two-year-old norteño accordion pioneer Narciso Martínez and filmed him at his day job feeding the elephants in the Brownsville zoo. Ramiro Cavazos, singer and guitarist with Los Donneños, a popular norteño group of the '50s, and owner of a McAllen, Texas, record store, helped Strachwitz and Blank meet Los Alegres de Terán, cornerstone norteño artists since their 1948 debut, "Corrido de Pepito."

In April 1976, despite having filmed the three great exponents of the music on the first trip, Strachwitz and Blank returned to Texas for more filming. Joining them on this leg of the trip was guitarist Ry Cooder, who had sought out Strachwitz because of his interest in Tex-Mex music. Strachwitz paid no attention to the rock world but was fascinated by another Anglo who was interested in this music, and he spent time playing Cooder his favorite Mexican 78s at his Berkeley hills home and yelling "yee-haw" until tears ran down his cheeks. Cooder heard about the filming and asked if he could come along.

In San Antonio, Strachwitz met with Genie Wolf, widow of Hymie Wolf, who had recorded many of the great norteño artists on his Rio label, and asked her who he should film. She enthusiastically told him there was only one musician in San Antonio who had the good looks and charisma to be a star, and his name was Flaco Jiménez. He was little known outside of San Antonio at that point, although Jiménez had played with Bob Dylan on a Doug Sahm session a few years earlier. He was the son of Santiago Jiménez, one of the originators of norteño conjunto accordion on popular records as far back as the '40s. They filmed Flaco teaching accordion to his son David, a third generation of Jiménez accordionists. In between takes, Cooder was sneaking lessons of his own from Jiménez.

Before going back to Berkeley, Strachwitz stopped in Lafayette, Louisiana, to record an important all-star Cajun record with D. L. Menard, Dewey Balfa, and Marc Savoy. The session was the Arhoolie recording debut of thirty-five-year-old accordionist Savoy, who would become one of Strachwitz's best friends and closest musical associates. Raised on a remote rice farm outside Eunice, Louisiana, Savoy graduated college with a degree in chemical engineering but decided instead to return home and make accordions. He was a wild man, an Elvis of the swamps, who played Cajun honky-tonks like the BO Sparkle Club in Beaumont, Texas, the last young man on a dying scene. Savoy started repairing accordions and then began to modify them. He soon was building his own unique models and opened the Savoy Music Center in Eunice in 1965, where the weekly Saturday-morning jam sessions with boudin sausages and beer became a central stop on the local music scene.

Balfa, a longtime Cajun fiddler who began recording with his brothers for Floyd Soileau's Swallow Records in Ville Platte after a triumphant appearance at the 1964 Newport Folk Festival, remained loyal to Soileau and declined to record for Strachwitz until this collaboration. D. L. Menard was often called the Cajun Hank Williams, whom young Menard had met at the Teche Club outside New Iberia, Louisiana, in 1951, shortly before Williams died. The trio had toured East Coast clubs in February 1976, and Menard was so enthusiastic about the session at the Savoy Music Center that he wrote a new song for the occasion, "En Bas d'un Chene Vert" (Under a Green Oak Tree). But Strachwitz's collaborations with Marc Savoy were only beginning.

MEXICO AND FLACO (1977-1979)

STRACHWITZ slacked his recording schedule considerably. He was through with the blues and infatuated with norteño music. He had worked his way through the Cajun field and, like Alexander, had no worlds left to conquer. In December 1976, he went into the studio with another wild card, the Klezmorim, a group of young Berkeley folk musicians who were playing old-fashioned Jewish klezmer music. They had built a following at the Berkeley folk music emporium Freight and Salvage, and after catching their act, Strachwitz was taken by the lyrical clarinet playing of David Julian Gray and spirited sax work by leader Lev Liberman. He had to work around a falling-out between the band and their Yiddish vocalist, Laurie Chastain, who insisted on being removed from the tape after the sessions. With her fiddle playing all over the tracks, Strachwitz compromised and took off her vocals.

In May 1977, on an abbreviated trip south while attending the annual New Orleans Jazzfest, Strachwitz brought Clifton Chenier into producer Allen Toussaint's Sea-Saint Studios in New Orleans and tried some more recordings with Texas barrelhouse piano man Robert Shaw in Houston that would stay in the can for years.

In January 1978, Strachwitz drove to Mexico to hear Mexican music in its native habitat. Many of the folk music styles of Mexico were enormously different from the norteño style. After driving down the West Coast and heading through Mexico City, Strachwitz landed in Veracruz, where one of his fellow folklorists was working on a doctoral thesis on son jarocho—the traditional music of the Veracruz region that blends elements of Mexican, Spanish, and African music, decorated with falsetto harmony vocals. As Mexico's main seaport on the Caribbean, Veracruz developed a distinct culture all its own. The best-known example of son jarocho is "La Bamba," a traditional Mexican folk song made into a rock and roll classic by Ritchie Valens. Strachwitz recorded Conjunto Alma Jarocha in the dining room of the hotel where he was staying. The band reflected the traditional jarocho instrumental lineup with two harps, a jarana (a small eight-string guitar), and a requinto (a ukulele-type instrument).

From Veracruz, Strachwitz continued north to the oil town of Tampico, where he was looking for a Huastecan fiddler he knew from old records. He asked around local cantinas and ended up in Boys Town (the red-light district) surrounded by mariachi musicians who insisted they could play the old music for him before sending him to another local bar. He eventually met vocalist Salvador Arteaga, who brought his band, Los Caporales de Panuco, to Strachwitz's hotel for a recording session, only to have management interrupt the session in Strachwitz's room and make him rent a ballroom downstairs to continue.

In April, Strachwitz brought filmmaker Les Blank with him to the New Orleans Jazzfest. After many years of trying, he had finally been able to convince producer Quint Davis to allow him to film Clifton Chenier at the festival. Unfortunately, Chenier insisted on using his own small and funky sound system that he thought would allow him to compete with Fats Domino. Instead, they dealt with catastrophic feedback and sound problems through the set. They were lucky to salvage one or two songs. He and Blank spent the next two months traipsing through backwoods Louisiana filming Cajun and Creole musicians for the film that would become *J'ai Été Au Bal* (*I Went to the Dance*), a film they hoped would do for Cajun music what *Chulas Fronteras* did for Tex-Mex. They backtracked over Strachwitz's old trails to shoot D. L. Menard, the Balfa brothers, Nathan Abshire, Canray Fontenot, Bois Sec Ardoin, Marc Savoy, and, of course, Clifton Chenier, along with many others.

Back home, as his recording schedule continued to slow, he finished a second album with the Klezmorim, recorded the last remnants of the San Francisco traditional jazz scene of the '50s, Dick Oxtot's Golden Age Jazz Band (most prominently employed at the time as strolling entertainment during Oakland A's baseball games), and a record with young white blues guitarist Tom McFarland, but otherwise he didn't return to recording until his trip south the next year.

In May 1979, once again around the New Orleans Jazzfest dates, he cut old-time Cajun fiddler Wallace "Cheese" Read in Marc Savoy's Eunice home, with Savoy backing him up, and tried out a friend of Savoy's, fiddler Wade Frugé, a lifelong amateur musician. In Crowley, Louisiana, Strachwitz ran some test recordings with a family of teenage zydeco musicians—think the Jackson 5 with accordions—called the Sam Brothers Five (Strachwitz had recorded their father in Houston years before when he first encountered zydeco), but ultimately made his album with the group two months later in a Berkeley recording studio.

In San Antonio, he caught a rare and inspired concert by Lydia Mendoza, who told Strachwitz she would be staying over for a few days with her daughter before returning home to Houston. He showed up that evening at her daughter's house with his gear, and, with Mendoza still riding high from the afternoon's performance, he recorded her spitting out nineteen songs, one after the other, in glorious voice. He also recorded one of the originators of norteño accordion, Santiago Jiménez, at his home with his son Flaco playing bajo sexto on the session.

The next day, Strachwitz made his first recordings with Flaco himself, although these initial recordings did not impress him. When he finished Flaco's Arhoolie debut in December at ZAZ Studios in San Antonio, owned by Tejano musician Joey Lopez, it was a different matter. While Strachwitz had still harbored some doubts about Flaco, El Rey del Acordeón, as Flaco was known around town, amazed Strachwitz in the studio with stinging, flying, fleet-fingered runs, red-hot accordion playing that Strachwitz had not heard from him at his dances, where Flaco downplayed his virtuoso techniques. Although Flaco had been touring as a member of the Ry Cooder band since Cooder met

CHRIS RECORDING MUSICIANS FOR *CHULAS FRONTERAS* 1975, ALONG THE TEXAS-MEXICO BORDER

For the 1976 film on norteño music, *Chulas Fronteras*, Chris served as producer and acted as the chief audio engineer.

him filming *Chulas Fronteras* and had appeared on *Saturday Night Live* with Cooder, this album would introduce the brilliant Tejano musician to a public beyond South Texas.

THE SAVOYS AND BEAUSOLEIL *(1980-1984)*

IF FLACO JIMÉNEZ represented a new generation of Tejano musicians, Strachwitz was also going to have to find young Cajuns carrying on those traditions into the future. Like the bluesmen, the old guys who made all those 78s were dying off. He was attracted to Marc Savoy, a good-looking, soft-spoken, fun-loving fellow with a deep love and understanding of Cajun music and lore. His Eunice music store was a touchstone for musicians from many miles around. With Savoy as his guide, Strachwitz would delve even more deeply into this fragile regional culture, under attack from the forces of modern society.

In May 1980, in between Jazzfest weekends, Strachwitz took zydeco primitivist John Delafose into Master Trak Studio in Crowley, opened by J. D. Miller, who made swamp pop and blues hits out of Crowley with Slim Harpo, Lazy Lester, Rod Bernard, and others, but it was now run by his son, engineer Mark Miller. Delafose, the forty-one- year-old son of sharecroppers, learned the button accordion as a youth and had been leading his band, the Eunice Playboys, at dances and roadhouses around the area for a few years.

The next week, after the second Jazzfest weekend, Strachwitz started recording with Marc Savoy at Savoy's Eunice home. The first sessions involved accordionist Moise Robin, a veteran of '30s 78s with fiddler Leo Soileau, along with D. L. Menard on guitar and Michael Doucet on fiddle. Strachwitz did not yet realize the significance of his meeting Doucet, a young musician who had studied at the feet of the Cajun masters, but he would soon learn. A couple of days later, twenty-nine-year-old Doucet returned to sing and play guitar on the first solo album by Marc Savoy, a loose, informal session that prominently featured vocals by a cousin named Frank Savoy, a funky backwoods character from Church Point who lived behind a beer joint. Also helping out on guitar and vocals was Marc's wife of three years, Ann Savoy, who would become her husband's closest musical collaborator.

Twenty-five-year-old photographer Ann Allen of Richmond, Virginia, had met Michael Doucet, who was playing with his Cajun rock band Coteau, and Marc Savoy, who was hanging out and jamming with Dewey Balfa and others at the National Folk Festival at Wolf Trap, Virginia, in 1976. She fell in love not only with the burly Cajun accordion maker but the entire Cajun culture. Within a year, she had moved to Louisiana, married Savoy, and begun studying Cajun history and culture for a book. A French student, she quickly learned to sing in Acadian and became an integral musical partner to her new husband.

Back in Berkeley, Strachwitz limited his recording activity to fulfilling a lifelong desire to record country star Rose Maddox, who was one of young Strachwitz's favorite acts on the radio growing up in Reno. Her once-illustrious career behind her, the country queen lived in Oregon and had been performing with a bluegrass band from the Sierra foothills, the Vern Williams Band, led by the mandolinist often called the father of California bluegrass. Strachwitz would have preferred Maddox in a more traditional country music setting, but like Clifton Chenier, she knew her audience and assured Strachwitz that this was the sound they wanted. He also had a brief encounter at Berkeley's Sierra Sound with Tejano maverick accordionist Steve Jordan, a norteño modernist who merged jazz, rock, and other progressive elements into his traditional sound. Jordan took the tapes home with him to overdub and Strachwitz never heard from him again.

In April 1981, on his way to New Orleans, he cut some tracks in San Antonio with Flaco's brother, Santiago Jiménez Jr. After Jazzfest, he met up with Michael Doucet to record Creole fiddler Canray Fontenot at his home in Welsh, Louisiana. The next day, in the sweltering heat of the Louisiana summer, Strachwitz conducted a session with accordionist Octa Clark and fiddler Hector Duhon in Michael Doucet's Lafayette living room—two Cajun music old-timers that Doucet encouraged Strachwitz to record. Doucet, who had intended to study romantic poets in graduate school in New Mexico, won a National Endowment for the Arts grant in 1975 and used the funds instead to study with virtually every master Cajun musician he could find. Clark had never been recorded, but Doucet's house had no air conditioning, so the energy may have been somewhat low.

Over dinner that night, Strachwitz proposed recording Doucet with some of the acoustic musicians he worked with in his progressive Cajun rock band. Doucet made the phone calls, and, within an hour, he had assembled his full crew at the chapel where he worked for the Bishop of Lafayette doing radio and TV programming. Like Clifton Chenier, Doucet cut a deal with Strachwitz—half the record could be the old-fashioned acoustic stuff Strachwitz favored, but the other half had to feature his whole band. They went at it without rehearsal, song list, overdubs, no time for anxiety. Doucet even had to borrow a fiddle because he didn't have time to go home and get his own.

The next day, everybody repaired to Marc Savoy's shop and recorded more numbers with Cajun fiddle great Dennis McGee. Dewey Balfa stopped by, and everybody ended up having a party in Marc and Ann Savoy's front yard. A few days later, they finished the album at Mark Miller's Master Trak Studio in Crowley and the first Arhoolie album by BeauSoleil was done. Like Savoy, Doucet belonged to a new generation of Cajun musicians, although Savoy considered himself more of a traditionalist. Doucet, who grew up in a musical Cajun family, played in rock bands as a youth and studied in France (where he was astonished to hear Cajun songs), so he knew the wider world beyond the bayous. He was starting to explore a vision of Cajun music that would eventually travel far and wide.

On his way home, Strachwitz stopped again in San Antonio to take Santiago Jiménez Jr. into the sixteen-track ZAZ Studios and cut seven songs, including "Corrido de Henry Cisneros," a song on behalf of the Latino politician currently running for mayor. He did little more recording that year and, when he did, it was not his idea. In November, Rose Maddox asked him to record an album of gospel songs with her and the Vern Williams Band after the death of her grown son that August. They went into Sierra Sound in Berkeley and cut the album in two emotional days.

In retrospect, the Savoy-Doucet Band seems inevitable. Fiddler Doucet used to visit their neighbors in Eunice, and the Savoys would join them for jam sessions and dinners. They started playing together regularly shortly thereafter. When they played Mardi Gras in Mamou, Louisiana, in 1980, the band caused quite a stir because there were few young musicians performing this traditional Cajun music and, right from the start, they were playing festivals in the United States and abroad.

Between the Savoys and Michael Doucet, Strachwitz had developed a new orbit in Louisiana. In May 1983, when Strachwitz returned for his annual tour of the bayous,

Doucet acted as a kind of talent scout for Strachwitz and he drummed up Rufus Thibodeaux, the Cajun fiddler best known for his long association beginning in the '50s with Grand Ole Opry star Jimmy C. Newman (he played on Newman's 1970 hit, "Lache Pas la Patate," the first gold record in Cajun French). Doucet and his brother, BeauSoleil guitarist David Doucet, backed fiddler Chuck Guillory at Master Trak Studio in Crowley alongside guitarist Preston Manuel, another old-timer who went back to the '40s. Doucet played mandolin. The next day, Doucet and the Savoys completed the first Savoy-Doucet Band album with Strachwitz in the Savoy's kitchen on his portable equipment.

In May 1984, in New Orleans for Jazzfest as usual, Strachwitz took his portable gear and two microphones to the treacherous Grese Lounge in the Tremé district to record the Rebirth Brass Band. Old-style New Orleans brass bands had been experiencing a revival in the city, led by the Dirty Dozen Brass Band, who wove modern jazz and funk into the traditional street parade sound. The members of Rebirth ranged in age from thirteen years old to nineteen years old—all former members of the J. J. Clark High School marching band—and trumpeter Kermit Ruffins would go on to become one of the city's leading musicians. At this point, they were just kids from the neighborhood, mixing New Orleans classics like "Lil Liza Jane" with Herbie Hancock's "Chameleon." The live recording was interrupted by an actual brawl after someone broke a beer bottle and went after another patron in an authentic New Orleans touch.

After Jazzfest, he went to Eunice to make a second album with BeauSoleil, who were beginning to actually sell records after becoming a favorite guest on the popular

RECORDING IN MICHAEL DOUCET'S LIVING ROOM
1981, LAFAYETTE, LOUISIANA

Chris made a memorable trip to Louisiana in 1981, recording Michael Doucet for the first time in his living room with Hector Duhon and Octa Clark. Chris learned the method of stacking the microphones from Mike Seeger. With each facing a different direction, this would help balance the volume of the accordion next to the other instruments.

public radio program *A Prairie Home Companion*. The band's progressive acoustic sound suited the homespun character the show aspired to, and BeauSoleil began to develop a substantial following. For the follow-up, Strachwitz accepted that he would be recording the entire group after he thought Doucet had sneaked in the rest of the band on the session for the first album. They cut twelve songs in eighteen takes. The next day, Strachwitz cut an album with Lawrence Ardoin, son of Alphonse "Bois Sec" Ardoin, the great Creole accordionist. He was originally the drummer in his father's band until his older brother's death in a car crash in 1974, when he assumed the accordion duties. Before long, his father had retired and he was leading the band and recording for Arhoolie.

THE LEGACY MATURES

TWENTY-FIVE YEARS AFTER the first Arhoolie album by Mance Lipscomb, Strachwitz surveyed an entirely different landscape in the folk music world, much of which he had a hand in changing. The audience for music in general had expanded so much that even the small pockets of blues, folk, gospel, and all the other marginal music could sell substantial amounts of records. Water rises in the lake, floats all the boats. The audience had grown not only larger but more sophisticated. Also, the availability of the music was much more widespread. There were dozens of small labels, little Arhoolies, putting out homegrown music. Rounder Records of Boston built the company into a thriving independent, accumulated a massive catalog, and sold millions of dollars' worth of records, including releases from many former Arhoolie artists. Even major labels began to traffic in this formerly peripheral realm of the music business.

The days of Strachwitz climbing over back fences to find some forgotten blues genius were over. In many ways, he was like a cowboy who rode the range contending with the coming of the automobile and his own obsolescence. He never stopped making records. He never stopped taking photographs, although as the digital era dawned, he moved from black-and-white to color photography and, eventually, videos. The most amazing thing about him—and there are so many—is that Strachwitz never lost his enthusiasm, never lost track of his bliss, and was always out there looking for the next big thrill. The lonely German kid who found such indescribable pleasure in old American records is still alive inside him.

In this new landscape, there would be Grammy Awards for Arhoolie releases (and eventually a lifetime achievement award for Strachwitz in 2016). Careers he fostered flourished. BeauSoleil exploded into a major act. Flaco Jiménez became a Tejano rock star. Del McCoury climbed to the top of the bluegrass world. The Arhoolie back catalog formed the foundation of an entire school of musical knowledge. There would be more awards and more documentaries, including one about Strachwitz, *This Ain't No Mouse Music!* (anything Strachwitz didn't like he referred to as "Mickey Mouse music," or, for short, "Mouse music"). His Austrian tour guide, Johnny Parth, specifically inspired by Arhoolie, started the comprehensive Document Records, producing an endless series of historic reissues under the more conducive European copyright laws. Strachwitz bought entire Mexican record companies and culled their tapes for compact disc collections. The label celebrated landmark anniversaries with gala concerts.

In 2016, Arhoolie Records was sold to a wealthy benefactor, who then donated the entire company to the Smithsonian Institution, which continues to operate the label. The dark, empty shelves on the ground floor of Arhoolie world headquarters look like the abandoned record company warehouse it is. The room is now largely reserved for buffets at parties. Up the creaky stairs, a large loft space is surrounded by book-shelves, groaning with books, magazines, and records. Piles of further material and boxes of records and tapes sit on tables. A row of filing cabinets contains publicity photos, prints from Strachwitz's personal photography, files of clippings, notes, old documents. On top of the filing cabinets are more boxes of papers and photos. In the center of this folk music situation room, a table is covered in file folders and stacks of photos. Strachwitz pulls up a chair to start thumbing through prints. Each photo seems to come with a story, refreshing in his nonagenarian mind the moment it was taken like it was only last week. These are pictures of a world gone by, but one that Strachwitz walked through with a tape recorder and a camera.

Lightnin', Mance, Clifton, Fred McDowell—they're all gone now. There won't be any more like them; the model is discontinued. These rare birds were sighted by Strachwitz when other people weren't even looking, and they laid down bedrock literature of American folklore. It turned out to be the last chance to capture these sounds, and Strachwitz was out there, largely by himself, collecting their stories, catching their songs, taking their pictures. He alone was Arhoolie, chief cook and bottle-washer, and he never had to answer to anyone else. He made the records for himself and, although the music belonged to the musicians, the vision was Strachwitz's.

Strachwitz went straight for the heart of American music. His unerring instinct for the genuine served him throughout his mission. He despised artifice and once chastised the formidable bluesman Howlin' Wolf for rolling around on the stage and engaging in bullshit. "Yeah," Wolf told him, "but people love bullshit." Not Strachwitz. He wanted to feel a musician's soul in his music, not marvel at contrivance or technical ability. He wanted truth and guts, not entertainment. If a musician couldn't connect to him on a visceral level, Strachwitz wasn't interested. Pop music, pointless and puerile, was beneath his contempt.

With those criteria, he sought out musicians who had been cast aside, both by the commercial music industry, who used them and disposed of them, and the community that surrounded them, as it moved away from regional culture. Mass media and corporate marketing spelled an end to regionalism, creating an artificial culture that can be mass-produced and mass-marketed. For much of the music he chronicled, if Strachwitz hadn't been there, it would be like it never was.

Strachwitz went looking for the real America. The people on his recordings sing this country's history. Their stories are the story of this country, all the joy and heartbreak, all the vaunted hope and dismal reality. It is all there in the music he collected, the songs he caught, the photographs he took—a portrait of America as rich, detailed, and truthful as any.

As much as the future cannot be known, the past is always with us. Strachwitz reached into a disappearing past and, before they were gone, took these pictures and made these records. In doing so, he preserved a way of life full of wisdom and hope for the future. Since he always approached these tasks with a guiding intellectual curiosity and a scholarly bent, the result was a well-organized inquiry into American music and the country that made the music. As much as coincidence and good luck played their

CHRIS AND VAN
1963, BERKELEY, CALIFORNIA

His Volkswagen microbus took Chris tens of thousands of miles in search of down home music.

part, Strachwitz compiling this body of work that encompassed the far reaches of the field was no accident but the product of a well-defined, brilliantly executed pathway.

All those thousands of miles behind the wheel of his car in pursuit of his vision showed Strachwitz an America nobody else saw. As the scrub trees and endless shrubbery of the Mississippi wilderness whizzed past his car window, the radio blasting some crazy preacher or mariachi music, he picked up the last vestiges of the old ways.

The world caught up with Strachwitz and the music he collected. Today, there is a drive to put up a statue of Clifton Chenier in Opelousas, Louisiana. Lightnin' Hopkins is revered around the world as one of the last great bluesmen. Flaco Jiménez is viewed as a national treasure in Texas, and there is a statue of him in San Antonio. The folk music Strachwitz celebrated has been spread in movie soundtracks, television commercials, every end of society, as music suffused the culture at the close of the twentieth century. In a computer-driven digital age, the appreciation of handmade, homegrown music has only increased.

As the corporate record business makes room for the music, they keep trying to find a category that works, a box to contain the uncontainable. They call it Americana or roots music. Some call it acoustic music, but isn't all music acoustic? Strachwitz was never in doubt. He always knew what it was—down home music.

PHOTOGRAPHS BY CHRIS STRACHWITZ

BILLIE AND DEDE PIERCE
1956, NEW ORLEANS, LOUISIANA

After I was discharged from the army at Camp Chaffee, Arkansas, I looked on the map and discovered that New Orleans wasn't that far. I got on a bus and headed to the city I had admired since I first saw that film called *New Orleans* in 1947, with Louis Armstrong and the whole Kid Ory Creole Band. I took a few pictures at Luthjen's Dance Hall, a small place that catered to Italian Americans who loved to dance to this kind of music. Of course, they played a lot of blues and stomps and all kinds of popular songs. Pianist Billie Pierce and DeDe, her blind, trumpet-playing husband, would later become quite famous via the Preservation Hall Jazz Band. Billie went back to the early blues era; she knew Bessie Smith growing up in Florida.

SLIM JENKINS'S PLACE
1959, OAKLAND, CALIFORNIA

On the Oakland nightlife scene in the '50s, Slim Jenkins ran the high-class joint where Duke Ellington, Nat King Cole, and Billy Eckstine played. He opened the first liquor store in Oakland the day Prohibition ended in 1933 and started the café and nightclub shortly thereafter. In those days, there was a thriving strip of nightclubs on Seventh Street. The Lincoln Theatre was on that street, and Jesse Jaxyson had his radio repair shop, where he made some of the funkiest blues and gospel records ever on his little label, Jaxyson Records.

MACK MCCORMICK WITH LIGHTNIN' HOPKINS AND LUKE "LONG GONE" MILES
1959, HOUSTON, TEXAS

This was my first day in Houston, after meeting Lightnin' Hopkins for the first time. I had received an amazing postcard from Sam Charters, whom I met while I was still studying at UC Berkeley when he was working on *The Country Blues*, the first book on the subject. I took off that summer from teaching at Los Gatos High School and literally took a pilgrimage to Houston to meet Lightnin' because I was just absolutely fascinated by this man—his voice, how he sang, what he sang about. This shot was taken outside Lightnin's apartment on Hadley Street, with blues scholar and local historian Mack McCormick and Lightnin's buddy Luke "Long Gone" Miles.

LIGHTNIN' HOPKINS AND L. C. WILLIAMS 1959, HOUSTON, TEXAS

Houston had no zoning laws or licensing requirements, so they had these beer joints in somebody's house in the middle of a block. They sold beer and cleared a space for the musicians. Lightnin's drummer L. C. Williams was singing; he was a good singer. The towel over the microphone was to avoid electric shocks because it was so humid.

MANCE LIPSCOMB
1960, NAVASOTA, TEXAS

After discovering that Mance Lipscomb was the local musician, Mack McCormick and I went to his house. At first, he wasn't there. His wife said he was cutting grass out on the highway and would be back around five o'clock. He turned out to be the most wonderful, polite person I've ever encountered. This is outside his little house on Washington Boulevard, with his wife and granddaughters. He's holding the guitar that I carried everywhere on that first trip. Jon Lundberg, who owned a music store in Berkeley, advised me to take an instrument because there were going to be people who either may not have a decent instrument or played only electric. I don't think Mance even had a guitar at all. He never called himself a blues singer. Of course, he sang blues, among a ton of other material. He called himself a songster.

JUKE JOINT
1960, MISSISSIPPI

On my way up from Baton Rouge to Memphis to meet with Paul
Oliver, I shot this place off the highway in Mississippi.

LIL SON JACKSON
1960, DALLAS, TEXAS

For my second time down there, British blues scholar Paul Oliver had sent me a list of people to look up. Lil Son was not on it, but I knew of him from his 78s, like the original version of "Rock Me Baby," and I knew that his name was Melvin Jackson from the composer credits on all his Imperial Records. Bob Pinson suggested we look in the phone book, which was from the '50s, and sure enough, we called the Melvin Jackson listed and that was him. He no longer played music, and he was, at first, reluctant, but when he realized we were interested in the history of all that, he became quite cooperative. We recorded some numbers right there, although he didn't have a guitar, so he had to use the Harmony that I brought along.

BUTCH CAGE AND WILLIE THOMAS
1960, BATON ROUGE, LOUISIANA

I met this amazing pair of musicians on my way to Memphis
to meet Paul Oliver. They were
discovered by folklorist Harry
Oster, who had been very active
in recording and documenting
a lot of the blues and other folk
music in that part of southeast
Louisiana. It was especially
wonderful to hear a black fiddler
like Butch Cage, a rare treat.

71

THE HODGES BROTHERS
1960, BOGUE CHITTO, MISSISSIPPI

I was always crazy about hillbilly music, which I first heard on the radio over XERB out of Mexico. On my first trip down south with a tape recorder in 1960, and on my way to Memphis to meet up with Paul Oliver, I wanted to meet the Hodges Brothers. I had been impressed by their 78 record *It Won't Be Long*, issued in 1952 by Trumpet Records, a label mostly known for blues run out of a Jackson, Mississippi, furniture store by Lillian McMurry. I had written to her and asked if she knew where I could find them, and she sent me their address.

They lived in Bogue Chitto, Mississippi, very close to McComb, which is south of Jackson, not far from the Louisiana border. After leaving Houston and New Orleans, I soon found myself in a rural area like I'd never experienced before. As I was approaching their address way off the main highway, I saw this mule walking in a circle and pulling a long piece of wood, like a skinny tree trunk. Two men there, the Hodges brothers, were apparently grinding cane. They lived with their mother in one of those shotgun shacks, raised off the ground in case of floods. Their mother got water from a well inside the house. She had to wind up a container on a rope. They didn't have a chicken coop. At night, the chickens would flutter up into the trees and roost. I couldn't believe poor people in America could live like this. This was a whole new world to me that I had no idea existed.

Since they didn't have any electricity, they suggested we go record at the radio station in nearby McComb, where the brothers also did regular broadcasts. I really was impressed by Felix, the fiddler, and he and his brother Ralph sang great together. Their other brother, James, simply played rhythm guitar. Their bass player was also their manager, and he worked as a disc jockey at the station, which is how we arranged to use the studio. I used my single EV 664 microphone. I stuck it on a mic stand and pointed it up so that it would pick up the sound all around them. To my chagrin, the bass player insisted on singing most of the songs, but since he was the one to let us into the station to use the facility, what could I say? You couldn't turn down your host.

BILL QUINN AT GOLD STAR STUDIOS
1960, HOUSTON, TEXAS

Gold Star was of course the label that Lightnin' would record for almost constantly. Lightnin' knew that whenever he needed any money, he could just go to Bill Quinn and make some records, so Bill was definitely one guy I was going to look up in Houston. He not only had that record label, but he also had a studio in his backyard. Actually, he had a pressing plant, too, for a brief time, and he told me that those big companies would never tell him how to make records. It took him a long time to set all that up. Then came a shortage of shellac during World War II. He would hold "biscuit days" where people would bring in their old 78s and he would melt them down to make new ones. Pretty funky-sounding sometimes, but a fascinating guy.

BLACK ACE
1960, DALLAS, TEXAS

I was becoming quite a detective. In Dallas, at a street corner where some Black guys were playing dominos or something, I went up and asked if any of them had heard of a guy named "Lil Brother."

"What do you want with him?" one said. They thought I was either a cop or a bill collector or something like that. "I like this record I have by him," I said. That changed his attitude. "He hangs out with Black Ace at a tavern around the corner," he said.

Now that excited me. Black Ace was on the list that Paul Oliver had sent me of blues players who had recorded in the '20s and '30s. This fellow told me that Black Ace came into this place every day by five o'clock. "You can't miss him," he said. "He'll have a white shirt on with 'Ace' written on his shirt." I walked into that tavern and that's how I met Black Ace.

BIG JOE WILLIAMS
1960, LOS GATOS, CALIFORNIA

Probably the single most powerful pure blues recording I was ever able to capture was the first session I did with Big Joe Williams in my shack south of Los Gatos. Using the single EV dynamic 666 mic a friend had loaned me, I caught the emotions and stress of his recent jail spell pouring out of him, his beat-up nine-string guitar and funky amp sitting on the floor facing him, creating that incredible sound feeding into the one microphone. His wife, Mary, who also brought their young son, sang on a couple of numbers with him. He had to have a friend drive him down from Oakland and back the same evening because he was still on probation, but shortly thereafter he took off with his family to parts unknown, probably New Orleans.

WADE WALTON
1960, CLARKSDALE, MISSISSIPPI

A worker wandered into the barbershop
owned by Wade Walton. Paul Oliver had
been given Wade's name as being a good
contact in Clarksdale, Mississippi. Wade
asked him if he played guitar. I recorded
the barber sharpening his razor while
bluesman R. C. Smith played behind it. It's
a fascinating record. I think a rooster crows
somewhere outside.

PAUL OLIVER AND JUG BAND SINGER WILL SHADE
1960, MEMPHIS, TENNESSEE

Paul was partially sponsored on this trip by the BBC. They let him use their amazing compact portable recording machine. He had made elaborate plans beforehand about who to meet and where to meet them. He got in touch with me because I was planning to take my first recording trip down there. We found all kinds of people. In Clarksdale, for example, we met the head of the local NAACP. I caught up with Paul and his wife, Valerie, in Memphis at the Peabody Hotel.

PAUL OLIVER AND LIGHTNIN' HOPKINS
1960, HOUSTON, TEXAS

This was the second time I met Lightnin'. Paul and I came down from Memphis via New Orleans and back to Houston, where, once again, Mack McCormick acted as kind of our host. I think having these earnest European fans seeking him out helped Lightnin' realize that there was a bigger world out there somehow that recognized him for what he was—an extraordinary genius of improvising blues.

WALLACE GERNGER AND PAUL McZIEL
1961, LAFAYETTE, LOUISIANA

On this trip my tape recorder gave out and overmodulated a lot of stuff, but it was also when I first captured the early beginnings of zydeco. They didn't even call it zydeco—they called it French music. Or La-la. Or Push and Pull. At a house party in Lafayette, McZiel was the accordion player and Gernger the washboard player. This was the old way, where they just took the metal out of a real washboard, put it in a frame, hung it around their necks, and scraped it with a bottle opener.

TRACKSIDE JOINT
1961, ROSENBERG, TEXAS

Typical beer joint area right next to the
railroad tracks in a small town about thirty
miles west of Houston.

BIG MAMA THORNTON
1961, SANTA CRUZ, CALIFORNIA

Somebody told me I needed to hear this singer at a bar in Santa Cruz, near Los Gatos where I was teaching. When I went there, of course, I immediately realized who she was. She had a big R & B hit several years before with "Hound Dog," long before Elvis Presley. There was a piano player, but sometimes even he would disappear. And there was a guitar player, too, supposedly, but he got too drunk and couldn't play at all. So there she was, hollering behind the drums, a band all to herself. She kept her harmonicas on the windowsill next to her in a glass of water.

BOB GEDDINS AND HIS DAUGHTER
1962, OAKLAND, CALIFORNIA

Bob was a super important early "record man" in Oakland who recorded Jimmy McCracklin, Lowell Fulson, and everybody else in the Oakland blues scene. This photo was taken at one of his many studios in Oakland. Every time I visited him, he had apparently either just got evicted, or the rent went up and he was working on building another studio. The guy spent more damn time and money hammering and sawing away. He was a wonderful Texas guy and loved the blues and gospel music. He put me on to Big Joe Williams. He was a huge encouragement and coach in the early days of Arhoolie.

MERCY DEE WALTON AND SIDNEY MAIDEN
1961, STOCKTON, CALIFORNIA

That was a little recording studio in
Stockton where I recorded Mercy
Dee. He had a big hit with "One Room
Country Shack" in 1953 on Specialty
Records. Mercy Dee was a fantastic
composer and blues pianist. I was still
teaching in Los Gatos when I met him.
Somebody told me about this weird
piano player in a roadside bar south
of Santa Cruz on the highway. When
I walked in, he was wearing a turban,
trying to be a cocktail lounge pianist. Of
course, he played one note and I knew
who it was. Nobody else had any idea
who the guy was.

PAUL TATE AND CAJUN MUSICIANS
1961, EUNICE, LOUISIANA

I happened to be driving back from New Orleans toward Houston on a Saturday morning and heard this funky-sounding broadcast emanating live from someplace. Although mostly in Cajun French, I understood it was coming from Lakeview Park in Eunice. I looked it up on the map and drove up there, and here was this amazing scene with the announcer on the left—a schoolteacher from Mamou named Revon Reed—and behind him was this elegantly dressed gentleman, Paul Tate, a well-known attorney in Mamou. He was also the captain of the annual Mardi Gras parade, which is a big thing; the captain leads all the horses. And he was very fond of Cajun music.

He approached me, knowing that I must be an alien from someplace else since I didn't look like the average Louisiana fan. He asked if I liked this kind of music and who I had heard. I mentioned Nathan Abshire as a wonderful accordionist I had heard on 78s. And he said, "Oh, you like the authentic music," by which he meant the music that was being played in the dance halls. He told me they were concentrating on traditional Cajun music, which basically people played only for house parties and their own enjoyment. He recommended I meet this fellow named Marc Savoy and gave me a phone number. The woman who answered the phone said he wasn't there but gave me another number. I called the second number and asked for Marc Savoy. He came on the phone: "Yeah, who is this?" I said my name was Chris and that I was from California. "Well, come on over," he said. "I just ran over two chickens, and we killed another one, and I'm making a big gumbo."

STAPLE SINGERS
1962, CHICAGO, ILLINOIS

The Staple Singers played on the first gospel show I ever saw in 1957 at the Oakland Auditorium. The people sitting next to me were as amazed at young Mavis Staples as I was. "That ain't no man—that's that little girl singing like that," one of them said. Record producer and blues fan Pete Welding took me with him to a church in Chicago where he was giving them an award, and I snapped this picture.

REVEREND OVERSTREET
1962, PHOENIX, ARIZONA

On my second trip to the South in 1961, a Black disc jockey took me to Scotlandville, the Black section of Baton Rouge near the airport, to look for blues singers. On that hot evening, I saw this preacher singing with his electric guitar and four kids preaching the gospel on the sidewalk around him. I was very much taken with him, but I had no idea what I could do with him—I was totally into blues at the time. The next year in Baton Rouge, I asked about him at the beer joint where he had plugged in his amplification system. The lady there told me his name was Reverend Louis Overstreet, and, the last she heard, he was on his way to Los Angeles but may have stopped in Phoenix.

On my way back across the country, I stopped in Phoenix and filled up my tank at a gas station in the Black section of town south of the river. I asked the gas station attendant if he had seen a preacher with four sons, and he told me his church was right around the corner. The next year, after recording an album with him at his church, I took the German documentary makers to film him as he took to the sidewalks of the wino district in Tucson, which is where I took this photo.

JOE FALCON
1962, SCOTT, LOUISIANA

Accordionist Joe Falcon was the first Cajun musician to ever make a record, "Allons à Lafayette," and "The Waltz That Carried Me to My Grave" in 1928. Somehow, I had met him, and he told me he would be playing a dance that night in Scott, which is outside of Lafayette. I almost got into a fight with these people at that dance. These two guys came up and surrounded me, heatedly speaking in this French patois I couldn't understand. Finally, somebody stepped up and told me they wanted to know why I was taking pictures, because they didn't want to see their picture in the newspaper drinking and having fun—if they were on welfare, they could get cut off. Once they found out that I was interested only in the music, and that I knew what an important person Joe Falcon was, they simmered down.

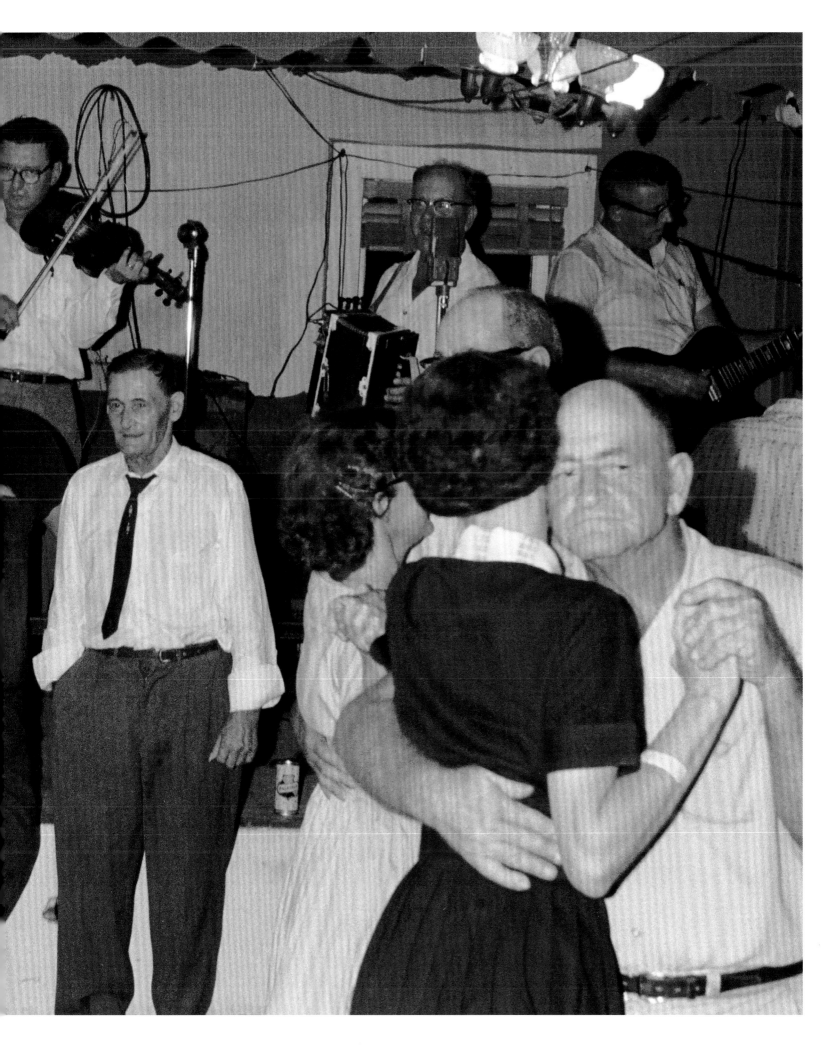

J. E. MAINER
1963, CONCORD, NORTH CAROLINA

He was an old-time fiddler who made a lot of records in the '30s that I always liked. I got his address in Concord, North Carolina, from Alan Lomax. I had met Mainer the previous year. He was a cagey old guy who had been around.

"Oh, you want my story, that'll be five dollars. Oh, you want my picture, too, that'll be another five dollars." Then I had to go buy him a pint of home brew in order just to talk to him. He was one smart dude who figured out how to make money off this damn guy. He wasn't ready to record, but I talked him into it and recorded him the next year.

PRESERVATION HALL
JAZZ BAND
1963, NEW ORLEANS, LOUISIANA

This is the beginning of the Preservation Hall Jazz Band, posing in the courtyard of the former art gallery where Larry Borenstein, pictured in the background, started throwing traditional jazz jam sessions in the late '50s. Allan and Sandra Jaffee, on sousaphone and drums, respectively, came to New Orleans on their honeymoon from Pennsylvania in 1960 and stayed to manage the club, hire the old-timers, and start the band, one of the great long-running acts of New Orleans jazz history.

**EUREKA BRASS BAND
1963, NEW ORLEANS,
LOUISIANA**

A New Orleans jazz
funeral featuring what to
me was the greatest of
all the brass bands. The
band goes back to the
'20s and has included
some of the great names
of New Orleans jazz over
the years. They knew
all the old spirituals and
dirges, as well as the
up-tempo jazz tunes for
the way back from the
cemetery.

LOWELL FULSON
1963, SAN FRANCISCO, CALIFORNIA

I escorted German filmmaker Dietrich Wawzyn to the Blue Mirror on Fillmore Street for him to film electric blues in an urban setting, although the Fillmore district was already in decline from its glory days before and after the war.

**KID THOMAS AND GEORGE LEWIS
1963, NEW ORLEANS, LOUISIANA**

Dietrich Wawzyn couldn't
afford the whole Preservation
Hall Band—I just wanted to
make sure to get clarinetist
George Lewis, my favorite—so
we had only a quartet to make
the recording for the film at
Preservation Hall. We did
arrange for piano player Sweet
Emma Barrett, "The Bell Gal," to
be on the recording, although
she is not in the picture.

LIGHTNIN' HOPKINS AND ANTOINETTE
1963, BERKELEY, CALIFORNIA

Lightnin' and his wife, Antoinette—the
"Frenchman little girl" who was also married
to someone else—on my front steps.

HARRY OSTER AND WILLIE B. THOMAS
1963, BATON ROUGE, LOUISIANA

Sitting by the banks of the Mississippi River, folklorist Harry Oster, one of the first scholars to document this music, and Willie B. Thomas, who accompanied fiddle player Butch Cage since the '40s but were not recorded until Oster discovered them in 1959. Thomas injured his back as a youth, which left him crippled and stunted his growth. Arhoolie later acquired Oster's Folk-Lyric label and reissued his historic recordings.

WILLIE GREEN AND DANCERS AT IRENE'S
1963, HOUSTON, TEXAS

This was a real wonderful beer joint in Houston, and this is definitely very early zydeco. Willie Green is the main accordionist there looking at me, while the accordionist next to him is just a seconding guy along with a typical little rubboard.

MANCE LIPSCOMB
1963, UC BERKELEY FOLK FESTIVAL

Our first Arhoolie album with
Mance didn't have any distribution and it sold mainly around
Berkeley record stores, but he
was invited to appear at the
annual Berkeley Folk Festival
for his first public performance,
before more than ten thousand
people at the Greek Theatre. He
handled it all like an absolute
gentleman and, when he returned
for an encore performance two
years later, he was greeted backstage by the folk music hero Pete
Seeger. He did amazingly well.

**MANCE LIPSCOMB AND HIS WIFE
1963, NAVASOTA, TEXAS**

I drove back with Mance from
California in my Volkswagen van
on that trip. After his debut at the
Berkeley Folk Festival, he would
come to the West Coast almost
every year.

LIGHTNIN' HOPKINS AND PHIL HUFFMAN
1963, BERKELEY, CALIFORNIA

Phil Huffman and his wife, Midge, played host to so many singers
at the time. He would give all these fantastic little dinners. Mance
stayed with him before I bought a house. Brownie McGhee and
Sonny Terry would stay there. Lightnin' stayed with him or with
some cousin of his. Phil Huffman was kind of our guru, a very
important person on our scene.

KING LOUIS H. NARCISSE
1963, OAKLAND, CALIFORNIA

His Highness had presided over the Mount Zion Spiritual Temple in West Oakland since 1945. He was quite a charismatic preacher and singer whose broadcasts used to reach far and wide. The sign behind the altar is his motto: "It's Nice to Be Nice." German filmmaker Dietrich Wawzyn was fascinated with sanctified preachers, and we attended several services for him to film. The women in the nurses' hats in the front were there to assist parishioners who might be overcome.

FRANKIE LEE SIMS
1963, BERKELEY, CALIFORNIA

Oddly enough, this is the only known picture of this fellow Sims, who made "Lucy Mae Blues" in 1953. He was a real sad case. A rural guy from Texas, he told me he was a schoolteacher, and I couldn't believe it. But it was probably true. A lot of those teachers in these regional scenarios, they didn't have any real degrees. They were hired because they knew more than the students. He is playing that guitar of mine because he didn't have one. This was taken in my apartment before I bought my house.

HACKBERRY RAMBLERS
1963, LAKE CHARLES, LOUISIANA

Hackberry was a dinky town south of Lake Charles where I went to the café and asked if they knew how I could find the Hackberry Ramblers. They were one of the original Cajun bands that started back in the '30s and were named after their hometown. I was directed back to Lake Charles and told I could find the home of founder and fiddler Luderin Darbone on Darbone Street a little north of town. I couldn't miss it, they said. I recorded them both at his house, where I took the picture, and at the Goldband Studios in Lake Charles, where Eddie Shuler was one of the few guys who made Cajun records and had known them.

BLIND JAMES CAMPBELL
1963, NASHVILLE, TENNESSEE

This was an amazing band that I believe I had met and recorded the year before. Somebody had brought me a tape when I was still teaching in Los Gatos. They were basically a Nashville street band that played every kind of music, but mostly blues, spirituals, country music, pop tunes, and old-timey music. It was a wonderful string band. They had two Black fiddlers plus a tuba and, of course, Blind James Campbell's singing and guitar playing. I wish I'd recorded more of them the first time around.

LIGHTNIN' HOPKINS
1964, HOUSTON, TEXAS

Outside Lightnin's apartment across the street was this grocery store. We took this shot after I made our best record together, Arhoolie 1034. I simply recorded him in his apartment with two microphones, him playing his electric guitar. I needed a good album cover picture, and he obliged. He was very happy with the session because he told me he felt more comfortable if it wasn't in a studio. When he was all by himself, he felt much more at ease to do everything that he wanted to. That was a wonderful record.

LIGHTNIN' HOPKINS AND BARBARA DANE
1964, BERKELEY, CALIFORNIA

Barbara was a fine blues and jazz singer who joined Lightnin' for an experiment of mine. We recorded them before a small audience on an afternoon at the Berkeley folk club the Cabale. I wanted to see if they could improvise together. Lightnin', of course, was a master, and Barbara Dane managed to a certain degree. It was an interesting session that became the second side of Arhoolie 1022.

BARBARA DANE AND THE LU WATTERS BAND
1964, SAN FRANCISCO, CALIFORNIA

"Blues Over Bodega" was a protest against PG&E building a nuclear power plant on the Marin County coast. Blues singer Barbara Dane, a political activist from way back, rehearsed the song with the great Lu Watters Band, who started the traditional jazz revival in the late '30s at San Francisco's Dawn Club, with Bob Mielke on trombone, Watters on trumpet, and Bob Helm on clarinet.

CLIFTON AND CLEVELAND CHENIER
1964, HOUSTON, TEXAS

I was in Houston waiting for Horst Lippmann to come from Germany to arrange for Lightnin' to go on the American Folk Blues Festival tour. I had finally talked Lightnin' into it. Before Horst arrived, Lightnin' asked me one evening to go hear his cousin, Clifton Chenier. I had seen Clifton before, but he was so loud, I hated it. This time, I heard it. It was kind of a typical beer joint, tiny little place with a low ceiling. He only had a drummer. He was singing incredible blues in this French patois. The first time I heard him, he didn't even have Cleveland with him. Cleveland used to play rubboard with Lightnin', and he may have made better money with Lightnin'.

HOPKINS BROTHERS
1964, WAXAHATCHIE, TEXAS

When Lightnin' told me his brother had got out of the penitentiary and was living up in Waxahatchie, I thought it'd be interesting to do something with the whole Hopkins family and Lightnin' arranged it. His mother drove with Lightnin', and I went up with Joel Hopkins, the one on the left, in my car. I shouldn't have let them drink, but, of course, they did, and they all got drunk. Lightnin' got really mean to poor old John Henry Hopkins, the guy on the right, although he had also said that John Henry was actually the best of all of them at making up songs and being a songster. What I got out of him was only a few weird things. At first, I didn't want to issue that record because it was so strange and chaotic.

FRED MCDOWELL
1964, COMO, MISSISSIPPI

I was so knocked out by the song he did on the Atlantic Records Southern Folk Heritage series, "Write Me a Few of Your Lines," that I had gotten Fred McDowell's address from musicologist Alan Lomax, who made the original recording. I went to the post office and they helped me find the route number address. As I drove into the yard at the farm, Fred was getting off a tractor. We made that record the first cold February night, the excellent Arhoolie 1021.

SONNY BOY WILLIAMSON
1965, HELENA, ARKANSAS

I first met Sonny Boy Williamson on the 1964 European tour by the American Folk Blues Festival, where I was hired to bring Lightnin' Hopkins. The following year on a trip down south, I went to Helena, Arkansas, where Sonny Boy had a daily broadcast on KFFA. I didn't know exactly where to go and was driving around the Black section of town when I saw a man coming out of a beer joint with a guitar case in his hand. I stopped and asked him, "Would you know where Sonny Boy Williamson lives?" And he told me exactly where to go.

Of course, the biggest mistake I made was not realizing who that guy was—he was Robert Nighthawk, the great slide guitar player. But I was so determined to talk to Sonny Boy to see if I could arrange to reissue his old records, it didn't even occur to me to ask the guitar player's name. Sonny Boy lived in a room behind the radio station. I hung my cheap mic next to the one the station used during the broadcast. Afterward I asked if I could take some pictures, so they set up their instruments in an alley behind the station, Sonny Boy, guitarist Houston Stackhouse, and drummer Peck Curtis. They were ready to pose because anybody wanting to take pictures was something unusual for them.

LIGHTNIN' HOPKINS
1965, NEWPORT FOLK FESTIVAL

He was always drinking his gin.
I went with him to Newport and
drank some apricot brandy, and
I got so drunk I couldn't get up
the next day when most of the
big acts appeared, including Bob
Dylan, who almost got knocked
off the stage. Willie Dixon and
some others walked back in the
barracks, where I was still laying
on my bunk trying to recover.
"Chris, you missed the big fight,"
Dixon said. "Who had the big
fight?" I asked. "Oh man, this guy,
Albert Grossman, and Dylan," he
said. I missed a lot of happenings,
but the next day I was functioning
and it was Lightnin' cooling
his heels.

131

BIG MAMA THORNTON
1965, AMERICAN FOLK BLUES FESTIVAL TOUR, GERMANY

In 1964, I went with Lightnin' on the American Folk Blues Festival tour, and the next year I took Fred McDowell. Big Mama was managed by someone else. Buddy Guy was also on the show. When we made that record in London on that tour, I taped a couple of numbers with only Fred McDowell and Big Mama. Gorgeous stuff. I wish I had done more.

Those are really three important people—Big Mama, Horst Lippmann (at left), and Joachim-Ernst Berendt (in conversation). Lippmann was one of the partners, along with Fritz Rau, but Horst Lippmann was the person who would get the artists. Berendt, the famous jazz pope of Germany, made this whole concert series possible because of his broadcasts on the southwest German TV and radio networks, who paid for the filming and put it on the air.

In 1969, Horst invited me to select many of the acts for the program, and it ended up being practically an all-Arhoolie affair: John Jackson, Earl Hooker, Juke Boy Bonner, Clifton Chenier, and Whistlin' Alex Moore—all Arhoolie artists—joined Magic Sam and Carey Bell from the Chicago blues scene.

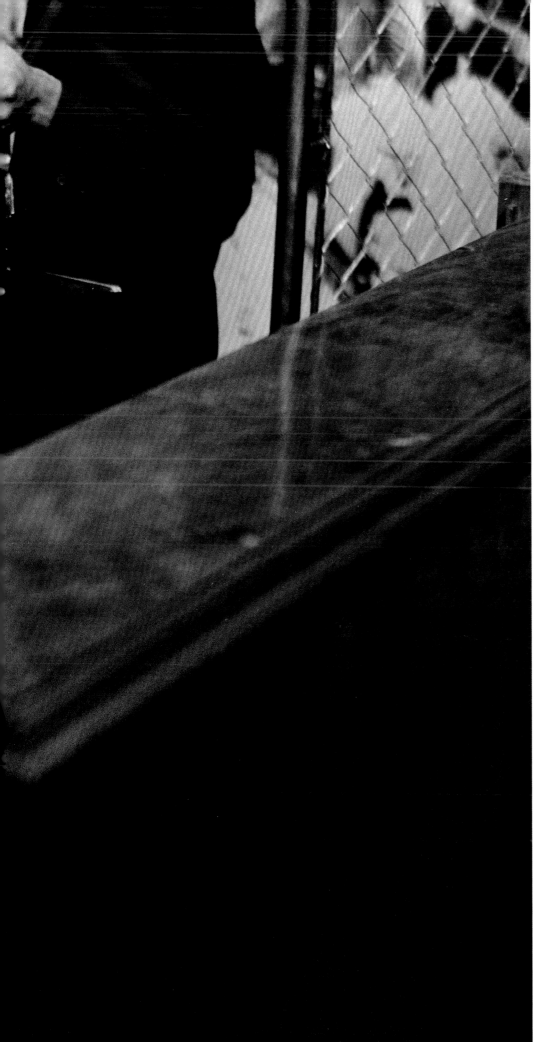

JOHN LEE HOOKER
1965, AMERICAN FOLK BLUES FESTIVAL TOUR, GERMANY

The Detroit bluesman first came to Europe on the 1962 American Folk Blues Festival tour and had been back to England several times when he joined the 1965 tour. I didn't really know him, but I couldn't resist taking this photo of the guitarist looking so moody sitting at the piano.

DR. ROSS
1965, BADEN, GERMANY

The one-man band at a television shoot during the American Folk Blues Festival tour. As a young man, he recorded for Sam Phillips and his Sun Records in Memphis but moved to Detroit, where he worked in the automotive industry the rest of his life. Left-handed Dr. Ross played a right-handed guitar upside down with the bass strings on the bottom. We called him the Flying Eagle because he used to stand up in the aisle of the bus with his arms spread while we rolled down the highway.

FRED McDOWELL
1965, COMO, MISSISSIPPI

On a warm, beautiful Sunday morning,
his friends and neighbors pitched an
impromptu party and Fred McDowell
provided the dance music in the front
yard. Everybody had come from church,
so they were all in their Sunday best.
I doubt I was as nicely dressed.

NATHAN ABSHIRE
1966, BASILE, LOUISIANA

One of my favorite accordion players outside his house. Nathan was one of the few I'd heard of before I went to Louisiana.

NORMAN PIERCE AT JACK'S RECORD CELLAR
1965, SAN FRANCISCO, CALIFORNIA

Norm was owner of this historic record shop and the first distributor of Arhoolie Records. We started out in his basement. I lived in the loft there for several weeks after I quit teaching in Los Gatos.

THE BALFA BROTHERS AND NATHAN ABSHIRE
1966, BASILE, LOUISIANA

The Balfas, one of the first Cajun groups I recorded, and Nathan Abshire started
recording Cajun music in the late '40s and early '50s. Abshire was by far the better
known. The Balfa brothers were happy to be playing on his record. Left to right: Rodney
Balfa, Dewey Balfa, Nathan Abshire, Basile Marcentel.

Joe Patek
1966, Houston, Texas

Through John Lomax, I had become quite fond of the Czech Bohemian bands that were all over South Texas. He told me about that music and suggested I tune in the radio next time I was driving back to California to hear this music. I loved the records that Joe Patek (far left) from Shiner, Texas, put out. He even put out a record called "Corrido Rock" with a Southwest feeling that didn't sound like those northern polka bands at all, much more western swing. This was a splendid dance at the Mraz Dance Hall in North Houston.

JOHNNY YOUNG AND WALTER HORTON
1967, CHICAGO, ILLINOIS

Johnny Young started playing blues
around Chicago in the '40s but had
retired by the time the blues renaissance
came around in the '60s. He was
a good mandolin and guitar player.
Walter Horton was one of the greats of
Chicago blues harmonica. Writer Pete
Welding helped make their Arhoolie
record. Johnny Young lived in some hard
conditions in the building where I made
this photo.

VARIOUS MUSICIANS
1967, AUSTRIA

These are from my first six-week trip to Austria with Johnny Parth as my guide to record Austrian folk musicians. We found some really authentic old-timers on that trip, including this street musician with his barrel pump organ, a brick marimba player, and these two farmers, not professional musicians, whom we recorded in the Vienna suburbs. They sang some wonderful Gstanzls for us. Those are kind of dirty songs.

JOHN JACKSON
1967, FAIRFAX, VIRGINIA

John played a remarkable combination of down home blues and hillbilly music that he
learned growing up in backwoods Virginia in the '30s and '40s. He was equally at home
with Blind Blake and Blind Boy Fuller as he was with Jimmie Rodgers and the Delmore
Brothers. He had long been out of music when he was rediscovered during the folk
boom in 1964. This was him and his wife at their home in Fairfax, the first time I recorded
him. He worked as a gravedigger and was another fine gentleman and songster.

DEL MCCOURY
1967, YORK, PENNSYLVANIA

I first heard Del two years before, when Bob Pinson and I presented Bill Monroe and his Bluegrass Boys in Northern California. He was one of the Bluegrass Boys at that time, and I totally got knocked out by that song "I Wonder Where You Are Tonight." I told him I wanted to make a record with his band just to get him to sing that song again. I don't know what it is—certain songs just grab me. I knew the damn thing had been around and was real corny, but he just had the sound. He is probably the most famous bluegrass musician today.

EARL HOOKER
1968, CHICAGO, ILLINOIS

I saw the Chicago bluesman Buddy Guy in Berkeley and asked him
if there was anybody in Chicago I should look for. He mentioned
two guys—Earl Hooker and John Littlejohn. Earl Hooker was totally
unknown beyond the South Side, but he was a fantastic musician.
He died young after suffering from tuberculosis most of his life; the
title track to his Arhoolie album *Two Bugs and a Roach*, is a remarkable talking blues about his most recent hospital stay. He was one of
those people who liked to play all kinds of music—especially country
music and blues and improvised things. Just extraordinary.

BONGO JOE
1968, SAN ANTONIO, TEXAS

This remarkable street singer was introduced to me by Larry Skoog, a big blues fan in San Antonio, although I also knew him well from a recording he did in the '50s called "This World Is in a Terrible Condition." My tape recorder wasn't portable, so I couldn't record him on the bridge where he played. I took some pictures before we went to Larry's apartment to make the record. Larry's son was with us. Larry also pointed me to an incredible collection of Mexican 78s later at the radio station KCOR. I made a special trip from Berkeley to buy records and came back with nearly a thousand, many very rare.

BACA FAMILY
1969, SOUTH TEXAS

Most of those Czech Bohemian musicians and families came from the part of
Czechoslovakia called Moravia. I put out a reissue of that music from 78s and called it
Texas Czech Moravian music.

AMERICAN FOLK BLUES FESTIVAL TOUR BUS
1969, SWITZERLAND

The bus on the tour where I helped put together the program. Arhoolie artists mixed with a couple of Chicago blues cats. Harmonia player Carey Bell sat across the aisle from Clifton Chenier. Alex Moore is sitting two rows behind Clifton, wearing a hat. Behind him, also in a hat, is Juke Boy Bonner, and Cleveland Chenier is behind Juke Boy in sunglasses. John Jackson is sitting in the back across the aisle in a cap next to the Swiss road manager.

ELM STREET
1969, DALLAS, TEXAS

Shades of Leadbelly and Blind Lemon Jefferson and "Deep Elem Blues." Most of the Black folks knew it as Central Track, where the action used to be.

BIG JAY MCNEELY
1969, LOS ANGELES, CALIFORNIA

A few of my friends were Big Jay McNeely fans—that honking music in the early '50s. That was kind of like what the Grateful Dead became to people so many years later. It was basically saxophone blowing with a solid 4/4 beat. I didn't realize he was one of the more sophisticated musicians of the idiom. This was taken at a private party in Los Angeles.

FRED MCDOWELL AND MIKE RUSSO
1969, BERKELEY, CALIFORNIA

Mike Russo was a discovery of Fred McDowell, who had met him in Portland, Oregon, where he lived. We did an album of the two of them together and another of Russo playing guitar and piano. He came down to Berkeley with Fred on one trip, and this was in my kitchen.

157

JOHN FAHEY
1969, MEMPHIS, TENNESSEE

The Blue Thumb Records gangsters had paid me to go to Memphis that year to record people from the Memphis Blues Festival. One of the young white characters that was around was guitarist John Fahey. I think we issued a couple of cuts by him, but we didn't use his name. I called him R. L. Watson. But anyway, he wanted to pose with those mules. I thought that was typical crazy John Fahey.

159

On a visit to Mance Lipscomb, I drove by this tin shack and pulled over to take a photo. They never called anything "blues," so Rock and Roll Cafe it was. I didn't stay for lunch, even though the door was open.

BUKKA WHITE AT MEMPHIS COUNTRY BLUES FESTIVAL
1969, MEMPHIS, TENNESSEE

Long after I taped *Sky Songs* with Bukka in my Berkeley apartment and at the Cabale Creamery, I also recorded him for Blue Thumb in Memphis. Later, I reissued all this stuff on Arhoolie because the guy never paid royalties to anybody, so we just took the tapes.

NEW ORLEANS JAZZ AND HERITAGE FESTIVAL
1970, NEW ORLEANS, LOUISIANA

The first New Orleans Jazzfest was a small neighborhood affair in Congo Square on the edge of the French Quarter. Clifton Chenier made a rare appearance in the city. Duke Ellington and Mahalia Jackson were there, although primarily the festival featured New Orleans musicians, food, and arts and crafts. There was a stage devoted to the traditional bands. They reconstituted the Sam Morgan Band, who had made recordings in the late '20s for Columbia, as well as the Kid Thomas Band. My friend Lars Edegran brought his New Orleans Ragtime Orchestra. It was mostly New Orleans traditional jazz bands. I don't think they had much rhythm and blues at all at that time, although the Meters did play. It was nice to see all this stuff together, this attempt to deal with the history that was still there at the time.

ANN ARBOR BLUES FESTIVAL
1970, ANN ARBOR, MICHIGAN

The second annual Ann Arbor Blues Festival was held on the grounds of the University
of Michigan and featured a roll call of the music's greats—Howlin' Wolf, Albert King,
T-Bone Walker, Big Joe Turner—alongside Arhoolie country blues artists such as Fred
McDowell, John Jackson, and Mance Lipscomb. Paul Oliver was an emcee. I went with
Mance. I caught Texas blues-rocker Johnny Winter meeting Mississippi Delta bluesman
Robert Pete Williams and a young Bonnie Raitt peeking out from backstage during the
Buddy Guy set. It was really fascinating—everything from country blues to the urban stuff.
All the good blues of that day.

LOS PINGÜINOS DEL NORTE
1970, PIEDRAS NEGRAS, COAHUILA, MEXICO

A young Mexican American activist/ student/composer/singer named Rumel Fuentes of Eagle Pass, Texas, took me across the border to the cantina in Piedras Negras where Los Pingüinos, led by singer/accordionist Rubén Castillo Juarez, often played. They were considered the city's primo conjunto and songsters. Los Pingüinos sang not only the widely known revolutionary corridos (narrative ballads) but were especially well versed in local and regional tales as well. I had my Magnecord 827 in the trunk and the audience was so wonderful, I wanted to record them right there. I asked the guy behind the bar if it would be all right, but he said no. He didn't want me bothering his clientele. We just went down the street a half block to another cantina. There was hardly anybody there and we did the album in a couple of hours—one song after the other.

While we were there, two girls walked in, which caused something of a stir because cantinas were for men only. But they had heard somebody was making a recording, and they wanted to be heard and sing. Over Rumel's protest, I let them sing a couple of songs. They weren't that great, and I never did anything with them. I took the photo, which ended up as the album cover, in the first cantina, not the one where we made the record.

BIG JOE WILLIAMS AND FAMILY
1971, CRAWFORD, MISSISSIPPI

After having done two albums with Big Joe Williams (including a classic early Arhoolie record I made at my shack in Los Gatos in 1960), I met up with him one last time in 1971 at his home in Crawford, Mississippi, where he grew up and where he posed for photos with members of his family.

BIG JOE WILLIAMS AND CHARLIE MUSSELWHITE
1971, BERKELEY, CALIFORNIA

Charlie and Big Joe knew each other from Chicago, when Charlie was sleeping in the basement of Bob Koester's Jazz Record Mart. Charlie worked for me packing and shipping records at the same time that his solo album was one of Arhoolie's bestsellers. This is the two of them fooling around on my front steps in Berkeley. There may have been some alcohol involved.

**BIG JOE WILLIAMS
WITH AUSTEN PETE
AND AMELIA JOHNSON
1971, CRAWFORD, MISSISSIPPI**

Big Joe Williams, who had
been around since the '30s
and was well known for
his "Baby Please Don't Go,"
acted as a sort of scout
for me. We made a new
record with him and several
of his local discoveries—a
woman named Amelia
Johnson, who I wasn't that
crazy about, a guitar player,
Austen Pete, and a couple
of others. Big Joe, of
course, did "Baby Please
Don't Go" for us.

HERBERSTEIN TRIO
1971, STYRIA, AUSTRIA

Johnny Parth was also my host for my second trip to Austria. I met him when I went to Europe with Lightnin', and Johnny got inspired. He not only started a record label releasing traditional Austrian folk music, but later expanded into the realm of Black American music, eventually founding Document Records in 1985, one of the most prolific reissue labels in the business. He put out an incredible number of comprehensive records, documenting Black music. Johnny had heard about this Herberstein Trio, a unique little group that played in this restaurant up in the Tyrol mountains. They also sang all these kinds of very risqué Gstanzls, suggestive and slightly rude traditional folk songs. But they played all kinds of stuff—hammered dulcimer, clarinet, and accordion.

MALY NAGL
1971, VIENNA, AUSTRIA

Maly was a well-known Viennese singer, associated with the Heuriger open-air taverns of eastern Austria, a rich tradition of special-license wineries where winemakers get to display the new year's crop. She made tons of records from way back, starting in the '20s, and had been performing on Viennese stages since she was a child. She was one of the real deals.

BOIS SEC ARDOIN
1971, MAMOU, LOUISIANA

When I went to visit the accordion player and his family at his home outside Mamou, they invited me to this nice reunion party. Typical Creole hospitality.

CLIFTON AND CLEVELAND CHENIER
1972, NEW ORLEANS, LOUISIANA

Clifton brought the bayou to the early Jazzfests in New Orleans, where zydeco was virtually unknown. He put his tie around his back so it didn't get caught in the accordion.

MANCE LIPSCOMB
1972, FRESNO, CALIFORNIA

Mark Spoelstra was a folk singer on the Berkeley scene who worked as a teacher in Fresno. Mance fascinated the kids in his class when he visited the school.

**PROFESSOR LONGHAIR AT JAZZFEST
1972, NEW ORLEANS, LOUISIANA**

I knew him for that one 1948 Star
Talent 78 by the Shuffling Hungarians,
"Mardi Gras in New Orleans." And he
had that hit in 1950, "Bald Head." I
was introduced to him on the sidewalk
of the French Quarter, but I was still
totally into traditional jazz.

KID THOMAS
1973, NEW ORLEANS, LOUISIANA

Kid Thomas started leading
bands in New Orleans in 1927.
His bands played for white
audiences in segregated
Louisiana, and their repertoire
spanned the full range of
popular music of the day—pop
songs, jazz, blues, waltzes,
whatever dancers wanted. He
and trombonist Louis Nelson,
who performed regularly at
Preservation Hall by that time,
appeared at the New Orleans
Jazzfest.

B. B. KING AND BUKKA WHITE
1973, NEW ORLEANS, LOUISIANA

His cousin Bukka was the first
bluesman B. B. ever heard.
He was the King of Blues by
that time, so B. B. joining his
cousin onstage showed him a
great honor.

TRIO SAN ANTONIO
1974, SAN ANTONIO, TEXAS

I loved that little trio—Fred Zimmerle on the accordion, Andrés Berlanga on bajo sexto, and the wild man on the string bass, Juan Viesca. Mike Seeger of the New Lost City Ramblers taught me how to record these guys. I had two Neumann microphones, one on top for the voices and the other one a little bit lower. That way I caught them singing and playing. It's not perfect, but I tried to do the best I could. We made some delightful records together.

NEW ORLEANS JAZZFEST
1974, NEW ORLEANS, LOUISIANA

Shake your booty.

BIG JOE TURNER
1974, OAKLAND, CALIFORNIA

Toward the end of his career, Big Joe often found himself being backed up by hippie rock musicians. It didn't matter who played behind him—Big Joe would just shout 'em out anyway. He was appearing before a slim crowd in the waning days of West Oakland blues nightlife at the Continental Club.

L. C. "Good Rockin'" Robinson, Jesse Fuller, and Tom Mazzolini
1974, San Francisco, California

Blues fan Tom Mazzolini presented the first San Francisco Blues Festival the year before on a rainy weekend at an abandoned UCSF gym. The second year, he moved to an amphitheater in McLaren Park, where it remained for several years with a bill featuring local blues talent such as Sugar Pie DeSanto, Dave Alexander, K. C. Douglas, and (pictured here with Mazzolini) Jesse Fuller and L. C. "Good Rockin'" Robinson.

Big Joe Turner
1974, Monterey, California

The blues great wearing his backstage badge at the blues afternoon concert at the Monterey Jazz Festival. The barrel-chested vocalist out of Kansas City was an impressive figure through five decades. Arhoolie later reissued some of his classic Swingtime 78s with boogie-woogie pianist Pete Johnson and his orchestra.

NARCISO MARTÍNEZ
1975, BROWNSVILLE, TEXAS

For the filming of the *Chulas Fronteras* documentary, I wanted Narciso Martínez. He developed a unique style that influenced everyone who followed. He was the father of Tejano accordion music. Narciso started recording extensively in the '30s for Bluebird, who issued his records under various other names (like "Polish Joe") because anybody who wanted polkas liked his music, and this gave his records wider distribution.

LYDIA MENDOZA
1975, SAN ANTONIO, TEXAS

Lydia was playing at a political rally for a candidate for mayor. He thought since the town didn't have any zoning laws, it didn't need any more beer joints in the neighborhoods. He didn't win.

LORETTA LYNN AND CONWAY TWITTY
1975, OAKLAND, CALIFORNIA

Loretta Lynn was one of those great country singers, and I have always been a fan. She had this great voice and sang about what happened in her life. After their show at the Oakland Coliseum Arena was over, they sat on the stage and signed the photographs that people had bought. It was a nice, friendly, down home scene.

FLACO JIMÉNEZ AND LES BLANK DURING FILMING OF *CHULAS FRONTERAS*
1975, SAN ANTONIO, TEXAS

I really admired the films that Les Blank had done with Lightnin' and Mance. Absolutely gorgeous movies. I asked him, since he had been documenting blues so well, would he like to take on this Texas-Mexican border music that I love. This accordion-driven music, with bajo sexto and the string bass usually, was the music of the whole region—not only South Texas but northern Mexico. That was the popular music that kept the working class alive in a way—truly functional music.

What he did with blues singers, I wanted to do with this music—to first capture the main recording artists who were still alive, like vocalist Lydia Mendoza and accordionist Narciso Martínez, who was practically the father of norteño music, and the hugely popular Los Alegres de Terán.

FLOYD SOILEAU, JOHN FOGERTY, AND ROCKIN' SIDNEY
1975, NEW ORLEANS, LOUISIANA

After Rockin' Sidney had a huge hit with his song "My Toot," John Fogerty came along and cut the song, which made it an even bigger hit. Floyd Soileau was the happy man who put out the record and owned the publishing. So that was quite a celebration on the Jazzfest grounds.

FLACO JIMÉNEZ, FLACO'S SON, AND RY COODER
1976, SAN ANTONIO, TEXAS

On that second trip, Ry Cooder and his wife joined us. He was especially keen about
Flaco. I met Genie Wolf, whose husband made his first records on the Rio label, and
asked her which of all these people I should record. She told me there was one guy who
could go places, a good musician, very handsome, looked good, and his name was Flaco
Jiménez. His real name was Leonardo, but they called him Flaco, which means skinny,
because he was fairly thin. I had heard him, but I hadn't realized how good he was. He
was definitely what was happening in the San Antonio area. He got involved and turned
out to be incredible. It was amazing how we had no trouble getting to all these people
who were so great, cooperative, and friendly.

**MARC AND ANN SAVOY
WITH D. L. MENARD**
1976, EUNICE, LOUISIANA

D. L. Menard was known as
the Hank Williams of Cajun
music. He met the country
music immortal when he was
working at a service station
and filled his tank. He asked
Hank how long it took to write
his songs. "It takes me about
a half hour," he told young
D. L. "If I can't do it by then,
I can't get it done."

BOIS SEC ARDOIN FAMILY BAND WITH CANRAY FONTENOT
1977, NEW ORLEANS, LOUISIANA

At the New Orleans Jazzfest, Bois Sec
Ardoin and fiddler Canray Fontenot are
two of the old-time Creole musicians
in the Eunice area who had been
recognized by various lovers of the
music as being great authentic players.
Canray was this amazing musician who
managed to send his daughter to college
on the wages that he made as a laborer.

FATS DOMINO
1977, NEW ORLEANS, LOUISIANA

At that time, Jazzfest was still focused on Louisiana and New Orleans instead of all these big superstars, and Fats was one of the big names that was appearing then. He certainly had huge hits, and I loved his music ever since I heard him in the early '50s.

CLIFTON CHENIER AND BONNIE RAITT AT JAZZFEST
1977, NEW ORLEANS, LOUISIANA

Bonnie has been a long-standing fan of down home music.

THE KLEZMORIM
1978, BERKELEY, CALIFORNIA

One of the sales guys from our distribution company turned me on to this wonderful Yiddish band. He steered me to the old Freight and Salvage in Berkeley, and I immediately fell in love with that music, especially clarinetist David Julian Gray, who, to me, was this most soulful guy. When they played those doinas, it was like the real blues. This is the band I did the second album with because they didn't have the trumpet, trombone, or drums on the first one. We're outside the Jewish Center in Berkeley.

TURK MURPHY AND BOB HELM
1980, SAN FRANCISCO, CALIFORNIA

I have always been a San Francisco traditional jazz fan. I love Turk Murphy. He kept that band running for years after the music had disappeared everywhere else. Bob Helm was a good clarinet player, a little bit on the scratchy high-end maybe, but he could play.

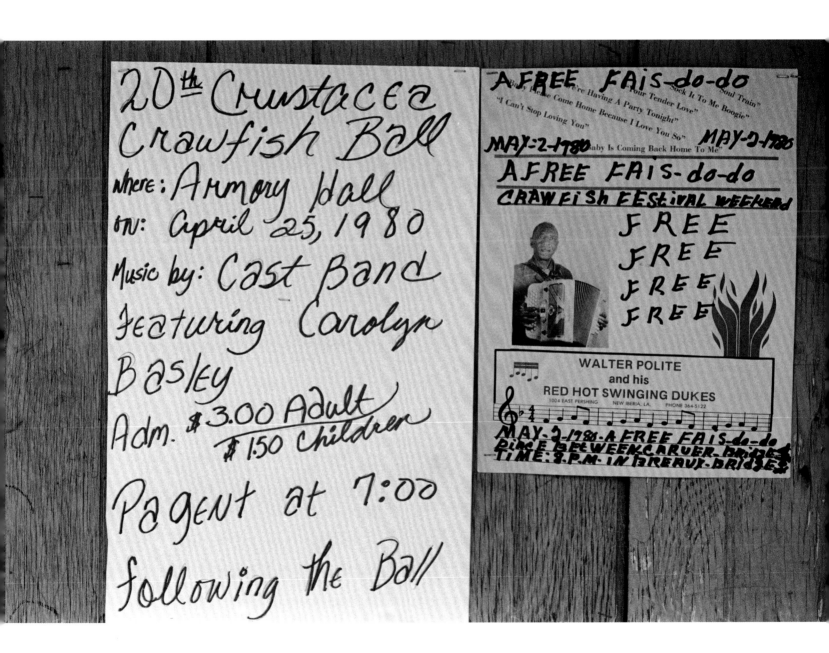

CRUSTACEA CRAWFISH BALL
1980, MAMOU, LOUISIANA

Posters on the side of the Mamou Armory Hall.

**SANTIAGO JIMÉNEZ JR.
1980, SAN ANTONIO, TEXAS**

Beautiful day for an
outdoor dance at the
Plaza in San Antonio.

BILL WHITE AND ROSE MADDOX
1982, BERKELEY, CALIFORNIA

Rose Maddox, of the Maddox Brothers and Rose, who had long been favorites of mine.
She and Fred were the only active remnants by the time I met them. The others had all
passed away. Rose Maddox was an incredible singer and pure country music. Bill White
was the ever-present Berkeley harmonica guy.

ROSE MADDOX AND THE VERN WILLIAMS BAND
1982, BERKELEY, CALIFORNIA

Vern Williams is the mandolin player on the left and his son, Delbert, is the guitar player on
the right. They moved from Arkansas and came to be known as some of the best bluegrass
people in the Bay Area. Ray Park was his sidekick on the fiddle, but this is later, when Vern
had started his own band and was going pretty strong in the bluegrass world here.

Flaco Jiménez and Chelo Silva
1983, San Antonio, Texas

Driving around San Antonio, I tuned to radio station KCOR, who were broadcasting live from the Conjunto Festival in Rosedale Park on the west side of town. I was amazed at the sound. Chelo Silva was the most famous of all bolero singers, especially from Texas, although she became known all over Mexico and the wider Latin world. Flaco Jiménez was just playing beautifully behind her. It was the most amazing performance, toward the end of her career. I put the microphone for my cassette machine on top of my car speakers as I was driving to the park. I caught about three songs before I parked the car and had to turn it off. But I later issued those three cuts.

LYDIA MENDOZA
1982, SAN ANTONIO, TEXAS

This was at an old folks' home, where she played her twelve-string guitar and sang requests. She knew more than a thousand songs and could sing anything they asked for. She would alter her guitar tuning if necessary. Her amazing repertoire covered the full expanse of Mexican music.

SANTIAGO JIMÉNEZ JR.
1982, EUNICE, LOUISIANA

He is one of the sons of Santiago Jiménez; Flaco is his brother. Marc Savoy decided he wanted to do a folk festival in Eunice, Louisiana. He formed a nonprofit called SPECIAL (Society for the Preservation of Ethnic Culture in Acadian Louisiana) and was keen about bringing this Tejano type of accordion music to people in Acadian Louisiana.

REBIRTH BRASS BAND
1984, NEW ORLEANS, LOUISIANA

I was very enthusiastic about the older brass bands. The Eureka Band to me was my idol because they still played the spirituals and the marches and the dirges and all that sort of thing. I heard about a young brass band—all teenagers— called the Rebirth Brass Band (which featured a young Kermit Ruffins on trumpet). There was a new wave of brass bands coming up in the wake of the Dirty Dozen Brass Band, who incorporated bebop and other contemporary music in their parade sound. There were three brothers involved. Their mother had to sign for them because they were all only teenagers.

LAWRENCE ARDOIN
1984, BASILE, LOUISIANA

This is at a small church hall in Basile, a benefit party where they had one group after another, with guests sitting in. This was a "French band," with Lawrence on accordion. It was a fantastic day of great music.

KEVIN WIMMER AND DANNY POULLARD
1985, RICHMOND, CALIFORNIA

Kevin Wimmer was a fine fiddler, originally from Berkeley, who moved down south. Danny Poullard was raised in Louisiana but didn't learn accordion until he moved to California and became well known around local folk music circles with the California Cajun Orchestra. They played these afternoon dances at some small club on San Pablo Avenue.

CARLOS SANTANA, ARMANDO PEREZ, AND FRANCISCO AGUABELLA
1985, SAN FRANCISCO, CALIFORNIA

Les Blank was filming the great Latin conguero Francisco Aguabella, and I went along with my Leica to take a few pictures.

LOS ALEGRES DE TERÁN
1985, SAN ANTONIO, TEXAS

Since their first record in 1948,
Los Alegres have been one
of the leading norteño groups.
They started in Mexico but
eventually settled in McAllen,
Texas, where they made records
of corridos, rancheras, all sorts
of norteño music, and were
always one of the most famous
groups in the area. Here they
are photographed at the annual
Conjunto Festival.

NARCISO MARTÍNEZ, LYDIA MENDOZA, AND VALERIO LONGORIA
1986, DALLAS, TEXAS

This amazing reunion took place at the Dallas folk festival that Alan Govenar organized—Narciso Martínez, the father of norteño accordion music; Lydia Mendoza, the queen of Tejano music, without doubt; and Valerio Longoria, who introduced the bolero into Tejano music. All three had careers that went back to the '30s and '40s.

STREET MUSICIANS
1986, GUADALAJARA, MEXICO

This blind harp player and his wife sang some of the old corridos on the sidewalk—
authentic street musicians trying to make a living.

MARIACHI MUSICIANS
1986, MEXICO CITY, MEXICO

In Garibaldi Square in Mexico City, all the mariachis and conjuntos would hang out to get hired. These guys played checkers while they waited.

VARISE CONNOR AND LIONEL LELEUX 1986, LAFAYETTE, LOUISIANA

Lionel LeLeux is on the left on the fiddle, Varise Connor on the right. Lionel played with Joe Falcon, the pioneer Cajun musician. Michael Doucet took me to meet these two old-time Cajun fiddlers. I recorded them for an album of Cajun fiddle music that Arhoolie never issued.

Ry Cooder with Flaco Jiménez
1986, Los Angeles, California

Ry tried to incorporate the
Tex-Mex sound in this unusual
band he led briefly in the
'80s with Flaco Jiménez on
accordion and saxophonist
Steve Douglas, a famous
Hollywood session man who
played on all the Duane Eddy
rock and roll records. Les Blank
was shooting a music video
for the band on a soundstage
in Hollywood.

Los Campesinos de Michoacán
1987, Redwood City, California

Redwood City was a hotbed for Michoacán music in those days, and Los Campesinos lived there. There were a lot of cannery workers in that area who came from the countryside in the state of Michoacán in Mexico. I made a nice record with them, too.

BOOZOO CHAVIS
1987, LAKE CHARLES, LOUISIANA

Chavis played for this big dance out in the country at the end of a trail ride. It was definitely a Black affair, all these Creoles who were really fond of their horses. They would get together and have these long group rides, with all kinds of barbecue wagons and always a big dance at the end. Boozoo Chavis was the attraction that day—fine Creole entertainment.

LES BLANK AND MAUREEN GOSLING
1987, SOUTHWEST LOUISIANA

During the making of *J'ai Été Au Bal* at a racetrack west of
Opelousas that is prominently featured in Les's film *Spend It All*,
with his editor-recordist and companion.

ROSE MADDOX AND FRED MADDOX
1987, MODESTO, CALIFORNIA

They were celebrating the fiftieth anniversary of their appearance at radio station
KTRB, where they started as the Maddox Brothers and Rose. They had this amazing
get-together, kind of a reunion, but at that time the only active brother was Fred, and
he was, of course, always the emcee. If you ever heard him talk, you could hear how he
could sell you anything. He had that great Southern drawl.

When he went to that station years earlier, they were starving to death in Central
Valley after they came from the South. He was tired of picking cotton and fruit—he said
he was "a-thinkin'" he would go see the radio station about playing music. The guy he
met at KTRB said he would only take the band if they had a girl singer. Fred said he had
one. Rose was about fourteen years old when she started with them.

FLACO JIMÉNEZ AND PETER ROWAN
1988, SAN ANTONIO, TEXAS

I liked Peter Rowan's song "The Free Mexican Airforce" and wanted
to record it on Flaco's next album. I cut it and some other songs with
him and Flaco's bajo player Oscar Telles, on the left, at the studio
where we made that recording in San Antonio.

WADE FRUGÉ AND WIFE
1989, EUNICE, LOUISIANA

Marc Savoy felt that Wade was the only one who played "Chanson de Mardi Gras" correctly—the old way. I recorded him on several occasions. He was a brilliant, soulful old-time Cajun fiddler who never played professionally but solely for house parties.

VALERIO LONGORIA
1989, SAN ANTONIO, TEXAS

Valerio Longoria and his son at the Conjunto Festival, an annual affair organized by Tejano music scholar Juan Tejeda that grew from humble beginnings into a major cultural event in San Antonio.

MARC AND ANN SAVOY
1990, EUNICE, LOUISIANA

I liked the way they looked at each other.

CANRAY FONTENOT AND THE POULLARD BROTHERS
1992, LOUISIANA

Canray Fontenot on fiddle, Danny Poullard on accordion, and Mike Poullard on guitar.

RICHARD THOMPSON
WITH MARC AND ANN SAVOY
1999, EUNICE, LOUISIANA

This is at a party in Marc and Ann Savoy's backyard. Richard Thompson, the British folk-rock musician, is with Nancy Covey, who always brought this fabulous group of people from Los Angeles into Cajun country during the week between Jazzfest weekends. They would always visit Marc's music shop, where he makes his accordions, and wind up with a nice party at his house, which usually took place on Tuesday. The night before, we would go visit Geno Delafose, where we would enjoy a great Creole presentation at the Delafose ranch just north of Eunice.

ACKNOWLEDGMENTS

The Arhoolie Foundation thanks authors Joel Selvin and Chris Strachwitz. The foundation applied the full weight of its resources to this project. Director John Leopold gave valuable direction and input. Arhoolie archivist Clarke Noone provided indispensable assistance. Arhoolie partner Tom Diamant offered advice, and his footprints are all over the massive organization of the Arhoolie archives. Adam Machado's Grammy-winning liner notes to *Hear Me Howling* and Elijah Wald's outstanding box set booklet for Arhoolie's 40th anniversary collection were both deep wells of information. Intrepid Lily O'Brien transcribed the Strachwitz tapes.

At Chronicle Books, thanks go to Nion McEvoy, Jack Jensen, editor Steve Mockus, designer Jon Glick, and the whole crew.

Author Joel Selvin thanks Chris Strachwitz, who brought him this project. One of the first articles to appear under his byline in the *San Francisco Chronicle* was a 1970 interview with Chris, and Selvin has followed Arhoolie and Chris as a journalist and friend through the years. Selvin salutes Chris as someone who stayed true to his code, stuck to his mission, and never lost the plot. He calls working with Chris on this book one of the highlights of his professional life.

Chris Strachwitz wants to send special appreciation to his great aunts Edith and Janet, who generously welcomed Chris and his family into their homes in Reno, Nevada, after World War II—a warm and loving environment where his passion for collecting old records was encouraged. Chris also wants to make known his appreciation for all the great musicians and offbeat characters he encountered on his life's journey. They were his true teachers.